D1603676

THE THEOLOGICAL SELF-UNDERSTANDING OF THE CATHOLIC CHARISMATIC MOVEMENT

James F. Breckenridge

University Press of America™

ACKNOWLEDGEMENTS

I would like to express my most sincere
appreciation to my wife, Lillian. Her advice
and assistance is a continual <u>sine qua non</u>
for our academic projects.

Also most deeply appreciated has been
the assistance of my typist, Ms. Gloria Frizzelle.
Her diligence and efforts have been a constant
example.

TABLE OF CONTENTS

ABSTRACT

The purpose of this paper is to examine whether the Catholic charismatic renewal truly represents the concepts and essence of Roman Catholicism. The exposition examines the self-understanding of the renewal in terms of Catholic thought concerning sacraments, charisms, communities, ecclesiology, ecumenism and the particular questions of Mariology and religious experience.

Relative to sacraments, one must distinguish between the crisis nature of charismatic religious experience and the progressive nature of Catholic religious experience. Charismatic theology brings a more personal dimension to the sacraments, but confusion results from usage of the term, "baptism in the Holy Spirit." Emphasis on the subjective perception of God seems to threaten Catholic emphasis on the sacramental life.

Possible reconciliation could be achieved by correlating the sacraments of initiation with a three-stage pentecostal experience. Baptism would equal salvation, confirmation would equal sanctification and the eucharist would signify the presence and power of the Spirit.

Relative to charisms, the Church certainly adopted a more charismatic theology at Vatican II. There seems to be a basic difference, however, between the more theological view of the Church as charismatic and the renewalist view of the individual as charismatic. The latter position seems to deviate from a theology of charisms which would be most supportive of the Church as an institution.

Covenant communities are by far the most controversial aspect of the renewal. The main question is whether they represent an "internal religious cult of renewal" or an "external sectarian movement of reform." Due to their composition of authority, institutional identity and religious experience, they seem to represent the latter. Accordingly, such groups seem to be spiritually, socially, and philosophically alien to normative Roman Catholicism.

Ecclesiologically, the renewal complements the de-centralizing influence of Vatican II. Definitions of the Church as a "sacrament," a "mystery," and a "people on the way" are congruent with charismatic themes. Ecumenically, the renewal has brought Council ideals from theory into the life of the parish, but in practice the renewal operates on the level of nondenominationalism. There is a question whether the renewal can maintain the dialectical quality of true ecumenism.

Some tension has been felt by Marian devotees who feel the Spirit has become an object of devotion which rivals the place of the blessed Mother. This in turn presents a question as to how the Spirit is perceived in worship. Do renewalists implicitly grant the Holy Spirit a cultic status which is tritheistic? Do charismatic perceptions in any way violate his revelatory and economic purpose in the Trinity?

Finally, the charismatic renewal has brought a spiritual challenge to the Catholic Church, but it has not been absorbed into the Church. The response of the Church to the renewal will have important implications for the future of all charismatic theology which seeks to address those visible and sacramental structures uniquely expressive of the Christian Faith.

INTRODUCTION

The purpose of this paper is to examine the extent to which the Catholic charismatic renewal truly represents the concepts and essence of Roman Catholicism. The renewal presents itself as a return to the dynamic of the Spirit which is an original and proper constituent of the Church. The validity of this claim and its consequences for both internal renewal and ecumenical purpose deserve careful consideration.

For Catholics, the renewal presents both a historical and a prophetical question. Does the renewal represent the Church of yesterday or the Church of tomorrow? And which of these is correct? Even more important, where is the individual believer in the post-Vatican II milieu? Does the renewal contain a principle of verification or interpretation which will serve as a true guide, or does it in fact lead away from the security of the Church to an essentially non-Catholic experience.

For Protestants, the renewal presents a theological challenge. The same religious experience exists in both Protestant and Catholic circles even though both have contradicting faith-systems. Should experience therefore precede doctrine as the cornerstone of unity? This also presents an ecumenical challenge--should the issues which divide really divide?

The study of these questions involved research of renewal authors, personal interviews with some central figures, attendance at two national conferences on the Catholic Charismatic Renewal and various personal encounters with members of prayer groups or communities. Perhaps more important for the author, the subject also demanded research of the Vatican II documents in order to understand something of contemporary Catholicism. This in turn brought a greater appreciation, charity and respect for the Roman Catholic Church, as well as instilling a permanent desire to know and understand more concerning the issues which still cause division.

Many sources are available for such a study; new books seem to be published almost daily. Not all of these, however, are of equal value. Well-written works that lend themselves to scholarly study are still rather few in number. There is also the problem of who truly speaks for the renewal and how seriously they should be taken. The first and second Malines Documents are certainly primary sources as are volumes by Suenens, Ranaghan, Martin, Clark, Gelpi, O'Connor, McDonnell and Ford. The personal interview with Rahner is of particular importance and interest. Any material from the early stages of the renewal can be profitable, but one has to ford works that are of the personal testimonial variety.

Kilian McDonnell observes that the charismatic renewal is the single most powerful force on the ecumenical scene today. "Both it and its ecumenical significance are permanent elements in the life of the Roman Catholic Church."[1] Accordingly, this paper seeks to address the renewal in a manner which will hopefully be a positive contribution to that greater understanding and unity which we all seek.

NOTES

1. Kilian McDonnell, The Charismatic Renewal and Ecumenism. (New York: Paulist Press, 1978), p. 113.

CHAPTER ONE

CHARISMATIC RENEWAL AND THE SACRAMENTS

Catholicism views religious experience within the context of grace progressively administered through sacraments. To discuss the charismatic movement, therefore, is to distinguish between the crisis nature of charismatic religious experience and the progressive nature of Catholic religious experience.

It is quite accurate to say that grace as process, ex opere operato, "covers" the Catholic believer from cradle to grave. It is also, however, quite accurate to note a general dischantment with the sacramental system, particularly the less central sacrament of confession:

Explain it anyway you like, lots of Catholics just aren't going to confession any more. Worse still, fewer and fewer Catholics seem capable of discussing the eclipse of the sacrament with even a semblance of rationality.[1]

To fill this gap, the Charismatic Renewal presents a crisis experience which adds new meaning to the sacraments:

The pentecostal movement flowing from the liturgy is not only radically incarnational but markedly eschatological. In it the risen Lord anointed is more fully present and active, more quickly coming to the eyes of faith. It is nothing which is not already celebrated in the official worship of the Church; it is but a deeper realization of this reality among the faithful. It is the actualization on the level of personal faith-in-action of the Christ-event we commemorate.[2]

1

The Spirit has deepened every aspect of my religious experience. I have found a new level of meaning in all the sacraments, especially in confession and the eucharist. I have come to a greater realization of the eucharist as sacrifice, and I have returned to frequent confession where before I was doubtful of its value as a corrective agent. I have found a deep devotion to Mary, and I can now praise God--something I had never been able to do before.[3]

Unanimously, people report a greater appreciation of the sacraments, especially the Mass as meaningful encounters with Christ, the Real Presence and the role of Mary.[4]

The existence of this new-found joy is reconciled to the sacramental system by positing a dynamic "openness to the Spirit" as a logical accompaniment or extension of Catholic religious intiation (baptism-confirmation-eucharist). It is pointed out that early Christians conceived of belief in Christ, participation in the sacraments and openness to the Spirit as "different aspects of a single, integral historical religious experience."[5]

If these early Christians were asked to locate the "baptism in the Holy Spirit," they would point to the celebration of initiation (baptism, confirmation, eucharist) by virtue of which the Spirit is imparted and received in his fullness. What the contemporary charismatic renewal calls "baptism in the Holy Spirit" belongs to the making of a Christian, and does not belong to a later, more mature stage of the Christian life.[6]

The problem is that Catholics do not seem to have appropriated personally the grace given in the sacraments. Ralph Martin observes that:

The sacraments of initiation are the "quality control" points which determine to a large extent the quality of Christian life in the Catholic Church. The life-giving Spirit of Christ flows into the Church through the sacraments. As they are currently administered, the Spirit indeed may be given, as sacramental theology tells us, but with virtually none of the effects that God intends them to bring about. They are certainly not producing a Church of vital Christians.[7]

Since renewal theology allows for the "revival" of a sacrament, meaning that inward dispositions may be released at a later period so that a believer may experience a subsequent "release" of the Holy Spirit into his life,[8] the charismatic movement in no way sees itself as introducing a contradiction into Catholic religious experience. Catholics who have not experienced a subsequent "fullness of the Spirit" are reminded that within the renewal movement this fullness or "baptism" of the Spirit refers to two moments. First, there is the theological sense in which everyone who has received sacramental initiation has received Spirit-baptism. Second, there is experiential sense in which the Spirit comes to consciousness at a later date.[9]

When Catholics speak of being "baptized in the Spirit," they usually mean the Spirit, given through the sacraments of initiation, breaking forth into conscious experience.[10] Kevin Ranaghan lists three basic steps by which the Catholic believer may receive this experience: (1) he must recognize the Son of God as Lord, (2) he must accept the pentecostal experience with a lively faith, and (3) he must accept and yield to the gifts of the Spirit.[11] Any or all of these requirements may be fulfilled anywhere--even in private prayer.[12]

It is also possible to receive the experience through the laying-on of hands at charismatic prayer meetings. This particular method, however, is criticized by some renewal leaders because it not only gives the appearance of an eighth sacrament,[13] but also represents a challenge to the episcopal authority:

3

To teach that the Holy Spirit comes through the imposition of Pentecostal (not episcopal) hands and not through the Sacrament of baptism is not a mere academic mistake. It has grave consequences for the whole movement, for the logical conclusion to this manner of using the texts is that non-Pentecostals do not possess the Holy Spirit.[14]

Those who persist in this manner of prayer insist that a sacrament is not being conferred, but that Christians who lay hands on a seeker are expressing an act of solidarity with the bishop who confirmed him.[15]

So then, the baptism in the Spirit, in spite of a sacramental title, is appropriated without regard to formula or liturgy. This does present the question of the exact purpose of the sacraments. If grace is conferred ex opere operato within the sacraments and subsequently "energized" from within at a later date, then exactly what constitutes meaningful religious experience? Do the sacraments become anterior to religious experience? Are they in any way subordinate to it?

It is impossible to deny that a considerable tension exists between charismatic reception of the Spirit and its sacramental counterpart. Simon Tugwell notes that:

When Paul bids us "preserve the unity of the Spirit," this unity is precisely given in the unity of baptism. If the Spirit is given in some other way more importantly than he is given in baptism, the unity of the Church is destroyed.[16]

Basic Catholic instruction teaches that the water of baptism is not only a symbol of the divine life, but actually produces it.[17] Further, that along with the divine life, Christ also gives us powers which "enable us to act as children of God."[18] Because of the graces given in baptism, the child of God not only is enabled to resist sin, but is also

4

expected to rise above mere observance of the law to a state of holiness. Baptism gives the "actual graces" which enable one to do this day by day.[19]

One way to resolve the confusion would be for the charismatics to change their terminology. Non-Catholic charismatics, for example, prefer to speak of the "fullness" of the Spirit rather than to use the more offensive term, "baptism of the Spirit." Renewal leaders readily admit that the latter term creates confusion, but they also maintain that more general terms present additional problems.[20] They seem to feel that opting for such a term as "fullness of the Spirit" denigrates the event-status of their experience.[21] Whatever has happened to them, it has changed their lives--it is something definite, an event in the truest sense. Any terminology which compromises its crisis nature will be rejected.

Interestingly enough, Kilian McDonell blames the terminological confusion on the classic pentecostals:

This problem is not really with the phrase "baptism in the Holy Spirit" but with the meaning now attached to that phrase as it comes out of classical Pentecostalism. There it is tied to a two-level (conversion-sanctification) doctrine of sanctification or a three-level doctrine (conversion-santification-baptism in the Holy Spirit). This doctrine of sanctification is essentially revivalist in character and is without a sacramental framework. The theological categories of Roman Catholicism are not revivalistic but sacramental. While Roman Catholics would look upon "baptism in the Holy Spirit" as another name for initiation, classical Pentecostals and many Protestant neo-Pentecostals would see it as a second (or third) experience subsequent to conversion. The problem Roman Catholics have with the phrase "baptism in the Holy Spirit" is not the phrase itself but the theological meaning it now bears

because of its use in the revivalist tradition.
It does not seem possible for Catholics to use
the phrase without implying the revivalist
meaning.[22]

What McDonnell sees, and what seems to be
the basic problem, is a root-level antithesis between the objective nature of sacramental grace
and the subjective nature of charismatic worship.
As one inclines to the subjective, there is a
deviation from sacramental grace as the foundation
of religious experience toward a more pietistic
view. Ford feels this is a dangerous bias: "An
inclination towards fundamentalism or a literal
interpretation of Scripture is extremely dangerous.
It is in the sacramental life that there are found
infallibly the fruits of the Spirit."[23]

The plain fact is that as long as Catholic
charismatics retain the term "baptism in the Spirit,"
a confusion will continue to exist. A number of
Catholics, overcome with the sensible experience,
reach a stage of skepticism concerning the validity
of efficacy of sacramental baptism and, occasionally,
repeat the rite.[24] The next step is to establish
themselves as critics who determine the authenticity of the spiritual experience claimed by other
members of their group.[25] "They then segregate
themselves from or ban those whom they do not regard
as reborn; and they quickly develop into a purist
or separatist group."[26]

When one approaches the question of infant-
baptism, non-charismatics object that:

. . .the effects of ordinary Christian
infant baptism are ignored or neglected in
favor of a basically unscriptural "Baptism
of the Holy Spirit" which is theologically
very confusing. Catholics know (as a matter
of faith) that a person who has received the
Sacrament of Baptism is now living a life of
grace which God in His ordinary economy simply
does not accompany with extraordinary phenomena.

6

Indeed, both the sacraments of Baptism and Confirmation are, in practice, relegated to second class status by the emphasis on a "Baptism of the Holy Spirit" considered as distinct from them. Some of our Catholic Pentecostals do not appear to understand that "the initial gift of the Spirit (in Holy Baptism) is none the less real for not being experienced or accompanied by charismatic manifestations; and that experience cannot be taken as the criteria of truly living in the Spirit."[27]

Charismatics reply that it is apparent that the vast majority of those baptized as infants do not appropriate the gift of the Spirit given in baptism:

The saving message, the kerygma, has not been effectively understood or appropriated by the Church as a whole. Countless millions of baptized Catholics in this country and others, have not personally committed their lives to Jesus, accepting him as their Saviour and Lord. Nor do they, despite the sacrament of confirmation, experience the effective power and working of the Holy Spirit in their lives. To sacramentalize or catechize in a situation like this can only produce a misshapen Christianity.[28]

More confusion results when one considers the sacrament of confirmation. Charismatics strongly feel that confirmation is often administered in a cultural situation in which "everyone is confirmed" with almost no regard for a basic commitment to Christ.[29] In the words of Ralph Martin, "It is heartbreaking to see 'The whole sixth-grade class' being 'prepared' for confirmation and then to see them 'receive' it with scarcely any tangible results in the way of strengthened Christian living."[30]

The concern is admirable and, logically speaking, renewal thought within classical Catholic theology would naturally focus on confirmation, which stresses the coming of the Holy Spirit upon the believer. The problem is that by stressing the subjective inward realization of the Holy Spirit, the renewal seems to negate the sacramental nature of the event.

An authorized Catholic instruction manual begins the section on confirmation by quoting Acts 2:1-11 and 8:5; 14-17. The point at issue is a desired spiritual maturity which comes not from growth, but "instantaneously, through the sacrament of confirmation."[31]

The Church was born from the pierced side of Christ on Good Friday; but it was not until the Holy Spirit descended upon her on Pentecost that she manifested herself to the world and assumed the responsibility of bearing witness to Christ. Somewhat the same thing happens in the life of a Christian. He is born into a new life at Baptism. He reaches his supernatural maturity, assumes his full responsibilities to bear witness to Christ when the Holy Spirit comes upon him in Confirmation.[32]

The statement is also quite clear that, "Through confirmation Christ confers on us the Holy Spirit, making us full-fledged and responsible members of the Mystical Body."[33] Further, that Christ's institution of confirmation is proved by the fact that he sent the Holy Spirit to strengthen the apostles, and by the fact that the apostles themselves administered the sacrament soon after the resurrection:

And Philip went down to the city of Samaria and preached the Christ to them. . . . Now when the apostles in Jerusalem heard that Samaria had received the word of God, they sent to them Peter and John. On their arrival they prayed for them, that they might receive the Holy Spirit; for as yet he had not come upon any of them, but they had only been baptized in the name of the Lord Jesus. Then they laid their hands on them and they received the Holy Spirit.[34]

8

The result of the reception of this sacrament is the very same power claimed by Catholics who have experienced the "baptism of the Spirit!" Let the catechism speak for itself:

Question: What is the effect of the distinctive character given in Confirmation?

Answer: The character is a _spiritual power_, [italics mine] a sharing in the priesthood of Christ. The baptismal character admits us to the Church and enables us to receive the sacraments and participate in the Mass. The character given in Confirmation consecrates a Christian for the defense of the faith and the winning of others to Christ.

Question: What are the powers which enable us to profess, defend and spread the faith?

Answer: These powers are the _gifts of the Holy Spirit_ and the _actual graces_ [italics mine] of the sacrament of Confirmation. These actual graces enable us to meet the challenge to our faith and to take advantage of the possibilities of spreading the faith in our every-day life.[35]

What renewal leaders do not see, or are unwilling to admit, is that charismatic religious experience is simply incompatible with sacramental religious experience as officially defined within the Catholic Church. Neither does there seem to be any logical solution.

Religious experience defined sacramentally is consistent with historic Catholic thought concerning man's spiritual condition. The Catholic view of the _imago dei_, for example, correlates perfectly with religious experience as offered in the sacraments. Man has suffered a partial fall, has lost communication with his Deity; it is through the sacraments that contact is restored and grace administered.

9

By appealing to an inward crisis experience, renewalists, albeit unknowingly, are presupposing a view of fallen man which is much more Reformed than Catholic--they are seeking a total religious experience which logically can be correlated only with a total fall.

An additional difficulty is that charismatic religious experience requires a completely different operation of grace. Catholic religious experience exists within a continuum of applied grace as opposed to the inward event nature of charismatic "infilling" grace.

At the same time, however, grace creates a strange liaison between Catholic and charismatic experience. Although each differs concerning the operation of grace, they are allied concerning the nature of grace. In both Catholic and charismatic worship, grace is imparted rather than imputed. In the religious experience of both, grace is quantitative in nature, capable of being measured and periodically administered. Worship assumes the character of address via sacrament or inward event.

The problem this poses for Catholic charismatics is that imparted grace assumes an adverbial character which at the same time both demands and prohibits adequate delineation of its locus within Catholic religious experience. Because it is imparted, it implies the question of its origin; but at the very moment an answer is proffered man becomes lost in a spiritual realist-nominalist tension. Is grace real because it comes from the sacraments or because it is existentially realized from within?

Renewal leader Stephen Clark states that:

When a person is baptized in the Spirit, the Holy Spirit not only comes to that person in a new way, but he also makes a change in him. His life is different because his relationship with God has been changed. God is in him in a way in which he was not before, He has made his home in him in a new way.[36]

Conversely, Josephine Ford maintains:

> It baptism in the Spirit is not a giving
> of the Holy Spirit or the establishment of a
> new relationship, e.g., becoming full sons and
> daughters of God, because all this is accom-
> plished in the sacrament of Baptism: to this
> Scripture bears unequivocal witness.[37]

The only way to solve this tension is by
an appeal to a unified concept of grace devoid of
such confusion. In historic Reformed theology, for
example, grace is imputative and legal in nature.
Worship assumes the character of response rather
than address; grace is sovereign and consequently
remains free and unified. Being realized through
faith, it does not question its origin and leaves
man without tension in its application.

A theoretical solution for Catholic theology would be to "pentecostalize" the Roman ordo
salutis by correlating the sacraments of initiation
with a three-stage pentecostal experience. Baptism
would correlate with salvation, confirmation with
sanctification, and the eucharist with the power
and presence of the Spirit.

By associating the latter with the Mass,
Catholic leaders would accomplish two things:
(1) they would underplay the "event" nature now
associated with reception of the Spirit, and (2)
they would undermine the divisive tendencies displayed by those who have reacted against sacra-
mentalism.

Such a solution, however, is extremely
unlikely. The classical pentecostal concept of
a three-stage religious experience is, as Kilian
McDonnell points out, essentially revivalist in
charater and does not have a sacramental framework.[38]

11

In the final analysis, there seems to be an irreconcilable conflict between the Catholic conception of the nature and function of grace and the charismatic concept of the work of the Holy Spirit. A reconciliation will have to take place or the Church will face severe disruption within its sacramental system.

NOTES

1. Donald L. Gelpi, _Pentecostal Piety_. (New York: Paulist Press, 1972), p. 3. In 1973 the Roman Catholic Church in the United States lost 200 priests, 2400 seminarians, and 3000 nuns. Catholic infant baptisms have dropped 31 percent since 1959; adult conversions by 49 percent. Seminary enrollment has declined 61 percent since just 1965. The divorce rate among American Catholics now almost equals that of the general population; many Catholics have apparently rejected the Church's teaching on abortion; the number of Catholics attending Sunday mass has dropped substantially. Ralph Martin, _Fire On The Earth_ (Ann Arbor: Word of Life, 1975), p. 10.

2. Kevin and Dorothy Ranaghan, _Catholic Pentecostals_. (New York: Paulist Press, 1969), p. 247.

3. Ibid., p. 70.

4. John V. McHale, "The Charismatic Renewal Movement," _The Furrow_ 24 (May, 1973):263.

5. Donald L. Gelpi, _Pentecostalism: A Theological Viewpoint_. (New York: Paulist Press, 1971), pp. 72-73.

6. Kilian McDonnell, "Holy Spirit and Christian Initiation," _The Holy Spirit and Power_, ed. Kilian McDonnell (New York: Doubleday, 1975), p. 81.

7. Ralph Martin, "Baptism in the Holy Spirit: Pastoral Implications," _The Holy Spirit and Power_. p. 103.

8. McHale, "The Charismatic Renewal Movement," p. 265.

9. Theological and Pastoral Orientations on the Catholic Charismatic Renewal. (Notre Dame, Ind.: Word of Life, 1974), p. 30.
10. Ibid., p. 31.
11. Kevin and Dorothy Ranaghan, Catholic Pentecostals. pp. 215-16.
12. Ibid., p. 216.
13. J. Massyngberde Ford, "Fly United--But Not In Too Close Formation: Reflections on the Catholic Pentecostal Movement," Spiritual Life 17 (Spring, 1971):13.
14. J. Massyngberde Ford, "Pentecostal Poise or Docetic Charismatics?" Spiritual Life 17 (Spring, 1973):34.
15. Gelpi, Pentecostalism. p. 181.
16. Simon Tugwell, "Reflections on the Pentecostal Doctrine of 'Baptism in the Holy Spirit,'" Heythrop Journal 13 (July, 1972):279.
17. James Killgallon and Gerard Weber, Life in Christ: Instructions in the Catholic Faith. (Chicago: Life in Christ, 1958), p. 162.
18. Ibid., p. 166.
19. Ibid., p. 167.
20. Theological and Pastoral Orientations. p. 30.
21. John and Jill Bowten to James Breckenridge, Nov. 11, 1975.
22. Kilian McDonnell, "Distinguishing Characteristics of the Charismatic-Pentecostal Spirituality," One in Christ 10 (1974:122-23.
23. Ford, "Fly United," p. 20
24. Ibid., pp. 16-17
25. Ibid.
26. Ibid.
27. James Likoudis, "The Pentecostalism Controversy," Social Justice Review. September 1973, p. 153.
28. Ralph Martin, Unless the Lord Build this House. (Notre Dame, Ind.: Ave Maria Press, 1971), p. 11.
29. Martin, "Baptism in the Holy Spirit: Pastoral Implications," p. 103.
30. Ibid.
31. Life in Christ. p. 175.
32. Ibid., pp. 175-76.
33. Ibid.
34. Ibid.
35. Ibid., p. 177.

13

36. Stephen B. Clark, _Baptized in the Spirit_.
    (Pecos, N. Mex.: Dove Pub., 1970), p. 15.
37. Ford, "Pentecostal Poise or Docetic Charis-
    matics?", p. 34
38. McDonnell, "Distinguishing Characteristics,"
    pp. 122-23.

CHAPTER II

CHARISMATIC RENEWAL AND THE CHARISMS

The historical Catholic understanding of charisms was the sevenfold conception of the Spirit and his gifts developed from the LXX version of Isa. 11:2. Specifically, they are defined as follows:

> counsel, the gift which moves us to act with prudence, especially in difficult cases,
> piety, the gift which moves us to love God as our Father and to have affection for all persons and things consecrated to him,
> fear of the Lord, the gift which moves us to fear offending God and being separated from him whom we love,
> fortitude, the gift which moves us to do great things for God joyfully and without fear of difficulties and obstacles.
> knowledge, the gift which moves us to see the things of this world in their true perspective, in their relation to God,
> understanding, the gift which moves us to a deeper insight into the truths that God has revealed to us,
> wisdom, the gift which moves us to judge all things, human and divine, as God sees them and to have a relish for the things of God.[1]

The sanctifying purpose of these gifts is to render the believer "docile to the inspirations of the Holy Spirit" as they mature from embryo at baptism to maturity through and following confirmation.[2]

With Vatican II, however, a new charismatic theology or view was officially endorsed. Interestingly, conciliar debate on the subject paralleled Protestant thought of the previous generation.

Cardinal Ruffini, in words similar to B.B. Warfield's, argued that charisms, though abundant in the apostolic era, gradually ceased.3 The ecclesial patron of the renewal movement, Cardinal Suenens, responded with the classical argument that existence of commonly accepted natural charisms justifies acceptance of preternatural charisms:

In reply, I pointed out that the charismatic dimension was **necessary** to the Church, I summarized the doctrine of St. Paul, which I have presented here, and ended: "What would become of our Church without the charisms of the doctors, the theologians, the prophets?": I also took the opportunity of my intervention to ask the Church to believe not only in the charisms bestowed upon men but also upon women, and that we should invite some women as auditors to the Council, if only to symbolize our conviction.
In regard to charisms, the Council adopted an open and receptive attitude expressed in a balanced text indicating that, provided necessary prudence be observed, charisms should be recognized and esteemed in the Church of today. Indeed we might add: they are more important than ever before.4

The Council responded to Cardinal Suenen's challenge with two main texts which afford conciliar refuge to the renewal movement.
First, Lumen Gentium:

It is not only through the sacraments and Church ministries that the same Holy Spirit sanctifies and leads the People of God and enriches it with virtues. Alotting His gifts "to everyone according as he will" (I Cor. 12:11), He distributes special graces among the faithful of every rank. By these gifts He makes them fit and ready to undertake the various tasks or offices advantageous for the renewal and upbuilding of the Church according to the words of the Apostle: "The manifestation of the Spirit is given to everyone for profit" (I Cor. 12:7). These charismatic gifts, whether

16

they be the most outstanding or the more simple and widely diffused, are to be received with thanksgiving and consolation, for they are exceedingly suitable and useful for the needs of the Church.5

Then, "On the Apostolate of the Laity":

For the exercise of this apostolate, the Holy Spirit who sanctifies the people of God through the ministry and the sacraments gives to the faithful special gifts as well (cf. I Cor. 12:7), "allotting to everyone according as he will" (I Cor. 12:11). Thus may the individual, "according to the gift that each has received, administer it to one another" and become "good stewards of the manifold grace of God" (I Pet. 4:10), and build up thereby the whole body in charity (cf. Eph. 4:16). From the reception of these charisms or gifts, including those which are less dramatic, there arises for each believer the right and duty to use them in the Church and in the world for the good of mankind and for the upbuilding of the Church. In so doing, believers need to enjoy the freedom of the Holy Spirit who "breathes where he wills" (John 3:8). At the same time, they must act in communion with their brothers in Christ, especially with their pastors. The latter must make a judgment about the true nature and proper use of these gifts, not in order to extinguish the Spirit, but to test all things and hold fast to what is good (cf. I Thess. 5:12, 19-21)."6

Both the language and the Scripture references of the above statements allow for a much greater emphasis on the preternatural gifts.7 Normally, however, Catholic theologians seem to view charisms within a more natural context relative to visibility and authority of the ecclesiastical institution. Karl Rahner defines the "dynamic element" of the Church in terms of its authority and recognition of that authority.8 In the Church itself

17

there exists "something historically irreducible and unique;" since this obviously comes from God rather than by chance, it follows that the Church must possess a "charismatic element."[9] Rahner identifies this as the mystical symbiosis of hierarchy and Spirit:

> All this is merely intended to make it clear that office and spiritual gifts in the Church cannot be conceived as two totally distinct elements which happen to be united more or less by chance in a person who is endowed with office and yet at the same time with a charisma. Office itself and not merely the actual man who in fact holds office must be characterized by charismatic gifts if the Church with its hierarchical constitution is to remain to the end the Church of the abiding Spirit.[10]

Hans Küng speaks of the "charismatic structure" of the Church as the creation of the Spirit in which men are freed from sin.[11] The Spirit is viewed as an eschatological gift, given to the Church at Pentecost, through whom all mankind receives the grace of God.[12] The charismatic "dimension" or "structure" of the Church therefore relates to the general spiritual function of the Church as it ministers to lives of believers.[13]

Although one senses that Küng might be more charitable to the renewal movement, the common denominator of both positions is charisms interpreted and applied within the visible Church. As stated in the Catholic Theological Dictionary, ". . . . the purpose of the charism is to make the Church visible and credible as the 'holy people of God', and thus it completes ecclesiastical office in its proper role."

Conversely, charismatic renewalists view charisms much more personally:

> A charism is an enduring endowment of the person which gives rise to experienced patterns of action, like the utterance of a prayer in

tongues or of a prophecy. But while it grounds
experience, it is itself pre-experiential. What
we experience is tne external patterns of action,
and we _infer_ from their regularity that they
proceed from an enduring endowment of the person.
That this endowment comes from the Spirit of
Christ must also be inferred from the impact of
tne supposed charism on tne life of tne individual in question and on the community at large.[15]

Ralph Martin speaks of "confirmation of the Gospel's
truth through the charismatic gifts of the Spirit
and the witness of full Christian community."[16]

        Two elements can be seen here: (1) charisms
are viewed as abilities rather than qualities, and
(2) as a "test" which indicates genuine Christian
experience. George Martin speaks of popes and bishops
performing miracles and being guided by prophecies
and visions.[17] In a charismatically renewed Church
the Spirit would pour out an abundance of every
kind of charismatic gift needed "on every kind of
person who could nelp," and pastors would be guided
by the Spirit to "discover with the instinct of faith,
acknowledge with joy, and foster witn diligence tne
charisms of tne laity."[18]

        The basic difference is that Catholicism
nas historically held that it is the Church that
is charismatic, not tne individual. Religious
experience is centered in the juridical reality of
tne visible institution and its ordinances. Within
such a context, charisms are meaningful only as tney
act in roles supportive of the outward Catholic
experience.

        Renewalists, reflecting tne tremendous
leveling effect of the decree "On the Apostolate
of the Laity," tend to emphasize the preternatural
and personal aspects of charisms. It is of interest
that Suenens' Vatican II speech appealed for inclusion
of laymen, women, and religious brothers and sisters
as auditors of the Council.[19]

19

The question is whether the individualistic and subjective emphasis of the renewalists can merge harmoniously with more institutional concepts. In at least three ways the renewalist concept of charisms seems to deviate from a position supportive of the institution: (1) there seems to be no satisfactory application of preternatural charisms to the ecclesiastical body, (2) there is no satisfactory definition of the relationship between natural and prenatural charisms, and (3) there is a question as to whether the renewal has truly conformed to historical Catholic norms for recognition of miracles or "outstanding" gifts.

Relative to the first issue, the position of Ruffini and Warfield is difficult to rebut when viewed in the context of historical Catholic theology. Ecclesiologically, it seems very difficult to make the Acts community normative. If one presumes, for example, that the Church is to have the same spiritual experience, then one should also expect the Church to have the same political experience (Acts 4:32). But what then should happen to the hierarchy? The problem is that accepting charismatic religious experience also means accepting charismatic hermeneutics. Any methodology which searches for norms in the first-century Church can easily assume an adversary relationship with a Church which finds its norms in tradition and evolution of dogma.

A possible answer would be to project the charisms in a role supportive of the institution. Protestants speak of a confirmation of revelation, Catholics of establishment of the hierarchy. Catholic scholar Josephine Ford maintains a New Testament succession for the hierarchy, but not necessarily for the preternatural gifts or charisms. Projecting the following chart, she calls attention to the continuity of the former and the cessation of the latter:[20]

20

50's A.D.	60's A.D.	6? or later A.D.
I Cor. 12:28-31	Eph. 4:11	I Tim. 3:1-12 Titus 1:5-6
Apostles	Apostles	Apostles
Prophets	Prophets	Prophets
Teachers	Evangelists	Bishop
Miracle Workers	Pastors	Presbyter (this may
Healers	Teachers	be the same as bishop)
Helpers		Deacon
Administrators		Deaconess
Speakers in Tongues		Widow (I Tim. 5:3-26)

The multiplicity of functions seems to diminish as time goes on. The functions primarily concerned with the fruits of the Spirit, especially love (care) and wisdom remain. Examination of early sources seems to prove that the Apostles were succeeded by the bishops, so that a line of succession could be traced through the bishops back to the Apostles and Jesus. This is necessary because the fruits of the Spirit as manifested in wisdom in teaching from generation to generation must always be preserved but the activities of the Spirit, such as, prophecy and healing are not indispensable; God gives when He thinks fit. There is no apostolic succession of these ministries.21

21

The implicit point in this projection is
the existence of a proper relationship between the
charismatic structure of the Church and the visible,
hierarchical order. The Church is the Body of
Christ; the Spirit is the Spirit of Christ. Consequently, the relationship of the Church to the
Spirit is the same as that of Christ to the Spirit.
Hence, the supportive role of the charismata is in
enforcing and defining the succession of hierarchy.
The rationale of the charisms and charismatic
activity will therefore be found solely in the
preservation and advancement of the ecclesiastical
body.

In point of fact, however, the majority of
renewal activity is taking place <u>outside</u> the
ecclesiastical body. Private prayer meetings and
healing of the sick, prophecy, laying-on-of-hands,
are all manifestations which seemingly have no
relation or application to the visible institution.
Renewalists have to explain how their charismatic
experience properly relates to and establishes the
Church.

The second tension point is the relation
of natural to preternatural charisms. Catholic
religious experience defines post-baptismal grace
in terms of personal sanctification. "God sends
. . .actual graces in order that we might perform
actions which will merit for us an increase of the
divine life."[22] The purpose of the gifts found in
Isa. 11:1-4 is to, ". . .render us docile to the
inspiration of the Holy Spirit" as they become
more fully developed through confirmation.[23]

Renewalists face the problem of relating
these admittedly more natural and institutional
gifts to the more spectacular charisms listed by
Paul. Renewal leader Stephen Clark chooses to
place them in different categories. He differen-
tiates between "spiritual" gifts (Isa. 11:1-4)
and "charismatic" gifts (I Cor. 12). The former
are intended for the strengthening of each in-
div..dual Christian, the latter for verification
of the Spirit's presence and work.[24]

22

Ford suggests another solution--she attempts
to distill Paul's gifts from the Isianic text:

> Summarizing our findings on I Corinthians
> 12:4-11, we find that to some extent these
> ministries manifest the gifts of the Spirit
> predicated of the "Messiah" portrayed in
> Isaiah 11:2ff. These gifts, as one recalls,
> are wisdom, understanding, counsel, might,
> knowledge, and fear of the Lord, the Greek
> Old Testament adding also piety. The utter-
> ance of wisdom and the utterance of knowledge
> easily fit into this pattern. The working of
> powers or miracles fits into the gift of might,
> although it is not the word dunamis, which is
> used in Isaiah eleven. Prophecy possibly fits
> into the gift of counsel; fear of the Lord has
> some affinity to discernment of spirits, and
> the gift of tongues and interpretation may be
> seen as part of the gift of piety (including
> worship).[25]

Neither solution, however, seems to be
sufficient. There is little warrant for dividing
gifts into categories of "spiritual" and "charismatic" as Clark has done. In Rom. 12:6-8, Paul
seems to mingle both natural and preternatural
gifts with ease. In no place does he attempt a
division between the two. His message is one of
a perfect blending between charisma and ecclesia.

Ford's position seems much too forced.
She distills Paul's nine charismatic gifts from
the Isaiah text by replacing the Catholic term
"fortitude" with the King James term "power" and
accepting the LXX addition of "piety." The
Masoretic term ＿＿＿＿＿＿＿＿ 7ﾠﾠﾠﾠﾠ , however, seems
accurately translated as the LXX has rendered
it-- _ἰσχύος_ rather than _δύναμις_.
The former conveys the idea of property and character rather than endowment, of quality rather
than gift. _ἰσχύος_ is the property, _δύναμις_
the accident. Also, it seems inconsistent to

23

change the flavor of the LXX term while accepting at the same time as obvious LXX addition, ενσεβειας.

The gifts of the Holy Spirit as normally understood in Catholic theology therefore seem incompatible with spiritual gifts as understood by renewalists. Any attempt at reclassification is frustrated by the Pauline penchant for synthesis. Any attempt at synthesis is faced by textual emandation seemingly contrary to the best Catholic tradition.

The final problem is that Catholicism has quite definite historical norms for recognition of miracles or supernatural manifestations. The question is whether the dynamic gifts claimed by the charismatics properly fit this historical framework. Karl Rahner makes the following analysis:

> . . . insofar as the charismatic movement is striving for genuine religious experience, contact with the Spirit and so on, that's a good thing and we have too little of that in the Church--and so in general that's a good movement.
> . . . But perhaps they are not in close enough touch with the spiritual history of the Church or the history of spiritual experience in the Church. Can they tie themselves into, say the history of mysticism, spirituality in the Church? Perhaps they have not done that enough.
> There's a long history in the Church of the critical evaluation of mystical experience, and they have not done enough of that with regard to their own experience; to evaluate, criticize, discern the value of a lot of this history. For example, the gift of tongues-- I would not deny that this could have a good effect or bear good fruit, but then the real value can also be overestimated. And then in the other examples, say, in the so-called cures, in the miraculous sense of sickness and so on, the Church has very well-established

norms for judging whether or not there was a
real cure here. Has the charismatic movement
applied these very strict norms to what they
are calling miraculous cures and healings?
Should they, for example, take the norms that
are used at Lourdes or the norms that exist in
canonization processes and so on? Perhaps
there would be fewer things that would be able
to be called cures than they are calling
miraculous cures.[26]

The point of Rahner's critique is that the
renewal movement has not declared the norms by
which it may be judged. The question is one of
validity versus reliability. The point at issue
is not whether the charismatic experience is a
valid religious experience but whether it is reli-
able. Spiritual gifts must possess both validity
and reliability. The latter element, conveyed
through the witness of the Church, answers questions
of authority, verification, history and purpose
which are essential to renewalist goals. No charismatic experience can remain uninterpreted for very
long. The renewal movement must define its purpose
and declare its norms in a manner which brings it
under the subjection, discipline and verification
of the visible Church. So far, such a restatement
or clarification relative to historic Catholic norms
has not been accomplished.

NOTES

1. James Killgallon and Gerard Weber, Life in
   Christ: Instructions in the Catholic Faith, p. 229.
2. Ibid., p. 177.
3. Francis A. Sullivan, "The Ecclesiological Context of the Charismatic Renewal," in The Holy
   Spirit and Power, ed. Kilian McDonnell (New
   York: Doubleday & Co., 1975), p. 123.
4. Léon Joseph Cardinal Suenens, A New Pentecost?
   (New York: Seabury Press, 1975), p. 30.

5. "Lumen Gentium" in The Documents of Vatican II. Gen ed. Walter M. Abbot, Trans ed. Joseph Gallagher (New York: Guild Press, 1966), p. 30.
6. "Apostolicam Actuositatem" in The Documents of Vatican II. pp. 492-93.
7. "Preternatural" refers to those gifts which exceed what is natural or regular. Such gifts would be abilities or aptitudes inexplicable by ordinary means.
8. Karl Rahner, The Dynamic Element in the Church. (New York: Herder & Herder, 1964), p. 47.
9. Ibid., pp. 8-9.
10. Ibid., p. 47.
11. Hans Küng, The Church. (New York: Sheed & Ward, 1967), p. 150.
12. Ibid., p. 163.
13. Ibid., p. 165.
14. Theological Dictionary, eds. Karl Rahner and Herbert Vorgrimler, trans. Richard Strachan (New York: Herder & Herder, 1965), p. 72.
15. Gelpi, Pentecostalism: A Theological Viewpoint, p. 202.
16. Ralph Martin, Fire On The Earth. p. 49.
17. George Martin, As The Spirit Leads Us. p. 245.
18. Francis Sullivan, The Holy Spirit and Power. p. 128.
19. Léon Joseph Suenens, "The Charismatic Dimension of the Church," Council Speeches of Vatican II. Yves Congar, Hans Kung and Daniel O'Hanlon, eds., (New York: Paulist Press, 1964), p. 34.
20. J. Massyngberde Ford, Baptism of the Spirit. (Techny, Ill.: Divine Word Pub., 1971), p. 24.
21. Ibid., p. 25.
22. Killgallon and Weber, Life in Christ. p. 26.
23. Ibid.
24. Stephen B. Clark, Spiritual Gifts. (Pecos, N. Mex.: Dove Pub., 1969), p. 7.
25. Ford, Baptism of the Spirit. p. 20.
26. Karl Rahner, Interview by Author, Jesuit Retreat House, Chicago, Ill., Nov. 7, 1974.

CHAPTER III

CHARISMATIC RENEWAL AND THE COMMUNITIES

One of the most controversial aspects of
the Catholic charismatic renewal is the existence
of para-ecclesiastical "communities" which are
spiritually, socially and philosophically alien
to normative Roman Catholicism. The central question is whether these groups, which conform to
early Hutterian and Bruderhof models, are indicative of an "internal religious cult of renewal" or
an "external sectarian movement of reform."[1] Many
critics feel they constitute the potential for a
very serious factionalism;[2] others, such as Catholic sociologist Joseph Fichter, maintain that
communities are, ". . . not counter-ecclesial and
only vaguely anti-institutional."[3] Because their
purpose is to stress "interior renovation of the
Spirit" as opposed to "institutional reform or
adaptation," Fichter feels they should be labeled
"an interior religious cult of renewal."[4]

Intelligent choice of either position
depends upon proper definition. The Charismatic
Renewal is an extremely complex sociological phenomenon, ranging from small, unstructured prayer
groups to large, highly-structured covenant communities.

Generically, the difference between the
two may be illustrated by the statement that,
"In a prayer group one shares activities; in a
community, one shares lives."[5] This is hardly,
however, a precise definition in that it does not
take into consideration the innumerable incremental
stages of "life-sharing." Between the polarities
of unstructured prayer groups and highly-structured
communities lies a complex continuum of social
groupings, each bearing its own unique relationship
to the Church. Small groups that meet in homes,
others in churches, some ecumenical, some exclusive--
all are to some extent involved in "life-sharing."

A more proper definition of a "community"
would be that of Bert Ghezzi:

> Prayer groups become communities when certain
> essentials develop. These include the raising
> up of men and women who perform the services
> of pastoral care for the community, of sound
> charismatic teaching and of leading people
> into the fullness of life in the Spirit and
> the community.[6]

Exactly what is involved in this definition
can be seen from an examination of three case
studies which Ghezzi has analyzed. The elements
common to each are: (1) visible leadership-authority,
(2) communal sharing of lives, at least to some
extent, (3) a religiously "open" atmosphere, (4)
organized instruction concerning the "baptism of
the Holy Spirit," and (5) the regular expression
of charismatic gifts.[7]

The seat of controversy resides in a few
(approximately ten in number) highly-organized,
ecumenical, "structurally consistent" (having
clearly defined interior patterns of authority and
leadership) communities.[8] Indeed, one feels that
the core of the controversy may involve an even
smaller number--the two predominent communities (the
People of Praise in South Bend, Ind. and the Word
of God in Ann Arbor, Mich.) which administer the
multi-million dollar operation of Charismatic Renewal
Services.[9] These most clearly demonstrate the
elements of covenant community while at the same
time displaying the formal bueaucracy necessary to
be considered a social movement--leadership, ideology,
a program, communications media, and a favorable
public image.[10]

Such selectivity could easily be mistaken
for academic fiat, especially when it is realized
that within the approximately 300,000 adherents of
the Catholic charismatic renewal in the United
States there are over 3,000 registered prayer groups.[11]
These, however, defy any attempt at labeling or
categorization. Although they report to the head-

quarters of the Charismatic Renewal Services, the only requirement for inclusion is that they be "predominently Catholic."[12] Indeed, the prayer groups are mushrooming so rapidly that the <u>International Directory of Catholic Charismatic Prayer Groups</u> is out of date as soon as it is published.[13]

These mushrooming prayer groups compared to the decreasing number of covenant communities demonstrate a phenomenon completely inexplicable to Renewal leaders. While the prayer groups, as expected, are proliferating, the communities, as not expected, are coalescing. In the 1969 treatise, <u>Catholic Pentecostals</u>, Renewal leader Kevin Ranaghan projected the following sequence:

> As a prayer group <u>develops more and more into a stable (though never closed) community</u>, these Christians united in the baptism in the Holy Spirit, will experience both the joys and the difficulties of community life. This has reference not only to the conduct of the prayer meeting but to the lives of the members in the larger religious and social communities under-lining mine.[14]

The July, 1973 issue of <u>New Covenant</u>, the official magazine for the Charismatic Renewal, observed that development of communities and "other groupings of Christians" appears to be one of the distinctive trends of the Charismatic Renewal. Further, that "growing covenant communities" already exist in Ann Arbor and Grand Haven in Michigan; South Bend, Ind.; Providence, R.I.; Rutherford, N.J.; Augusta, Ga.; Minneapolis, Minn.; and San Francisco, Calif.[15] In 1971 Bert Ghezzi observed that, "Most of the successful prayer groups have decided at some point to become more than a prayer group. To pledge themselves corporately to become as perfect as possible a local incarnation of the body of

29

Christ [sic] ."16 He concluded by saying:

> The calling together of a particular people,
> of a local manifestation of the body of Christ,
> is a fresh new thing God himself is doing. He
> is repeopling the face of the earth. Through-
> out the North American continent there are
> hundreds of sister communities to the three
> described here [Ghezzi's three case studies] --
> from Regina, Saskatchewan to Hollywood, Florida.17

Logical expectations of charismatic pro-
jections would foresee not one or ten communities
but hundreds, developing from their seed-bed prayer
groups. The goal of the Renewal was not "simply
to form small groups of Christians for prayer in the
Spirit, but to form full Christian communities."18

Paradoxically, just the opposite has
happened. The San Francisco community of John the
Baptist mentioned by Ghezzi has moved en masse from
California to merge with the People of Praise in
South Bend. Former Head Coordinatory of John the
Baptist, Kerry Kohler, explains: "We came here be-
cause we just couldn't cut the way of life in San
Francisco. People were widely separated and the
general social milieu was just not conducive to a
separated way of life."19

One community, the Children of Joy, in
Allentown, Pennsylvania, was dissolved by order
of the bishop.20 Another South Bend community,
True House, merged with the People of Praise when
instructed by the bishop to remove its leader for
objectionable practices, "or else."21 At the 1975
Charismatic Renewal Convention press conference
concerning communities, only four covenant communities were represented; discussion centered solely
around these with no mention of smaller, exclusively
Roman Catholic groups.22

The attitudes of Renewal leaders also seem
to fluctuate. Kerry Kohler asserts that prayer
groups are absolutely not expected to expand into

30

covenant communities.[23] George Martin cautions:

No set of principles comprise the blueprint to
success. No prayer group can identically dup-
licate any other group's "success story" . . .
in the final analysis, the path of the Lord
for each group and each parish must be in-
dividually discerned.[24]

Obviously, some change has taken place.
J. Massyngberde Ford, a disenchanted charismatic
scholar, sees the covenant communities as being
theologically deviant. In Which Way Catholic
Pentecostals?, she classifies the communities as
"Type I" charismatic manifestations synonymous
with historic Anabaptist spirituality.[25] Such
religious experience is exemplified in Zwingli
and Agricola, and is further defined in the ordinances predicated of the "true church" by
Dietrich Phillips.[26] "Type I" charismatics dis-
play a para-ecclesial structure consisting of
teachings, advisories, an excutive magisterium
and a disciplinary system.[27] Such spirituality
is symptomatic of the "pure community" concept,
advocating such practices as believer's baptism,
baptism of the Spirit, separation, washing of
feet and community of goods accompanied by clearly
defined authority figures."[28]

The smaller unstructured or exclusively
Catholic communities are labeled by Ford as
"Type II" Catholic pentecostals, representing a
religious experience that is "fully integrated
with the theology and sacramentality of the contemporary Catholic Church."[29] This type is exemplified by more ecclesial groups such as Benet
Lake Benedictine Monastery and some university
and private groups.[30] "Type II" Catholic pentecostals show extreme flexibility and little structure.[31] Their spirituality is "church-centered
with community and covenant confirmed through
liturgy."[32] Rather than stressing tongues, worship
involves the classical "aids to contemplation" such

31

as the Rosary and liturgical prayers.[33]

Many of Ford's criticisms are accurate and
deserved. The association of "Type I" charismatics
witn Anabaptist spirituality seems proper, as does
ner appreciation for the more "ecclesial" groups.
The work can be faulted, nowever, for its refusal
to discriminate further between "classes" of charismatics. Why only two classes? Would there not be
room for many sucn categories? Possible divisions
would be university groups, ecclesial groups, monastic, clerical, lay and parish groups. There seems
to be no reason why there would not be multiple
classifications.

Further, one must be reminded of Ford's
basic motive. An ardent feminist, sne was banned
from the Soutn Bend communities because of severe
conflicts with the male leadership.[34] In rem-
iniscing about tne movement's beginnings, sne states
that, "This was a changing group with no leadership
save Jesus and no catechumenate . . . italics
mine ."[35] Further that, "This teaching of subordination, adopted by the covenant groups, has been
a great impediment to women in the pentecostal
movement . . ."[36] "Type I Pentecostals nave worked
out an elaborate community structure which depends
largely upon the unquestioning submission of the
majority to male members."[37] She further notes
that tne New Testament "elder" structure followed
by all main-line communities is expressive of a
movement that is organized and authoritarian.[38]

One senses that the controversy over male
autnority is a slight misdirection of the central
question. Catholicism nas always espoused a strong
male hierarchy. Monastic groups historically dis-
play not only strong authority patterns, but also
many ingredients labeled by Ford as "anabaptistic."
St. Anthony was certainly a charismatic leader;
Athanasius advocates tne forsaking of temporal goods,
the sacredness of nature and tne pursuit of personal

32

faith over reason.[39] John Cassian extols subjective religious experience and attainment of inner purity.[40] St. Benedict warns of severe punishment by superiors and cautions that "no one may follow the will of his own heart."[41] The elements of mysticism, authority and male leadership are common to proper Catholic experience.

The tension seems more properly defined as a philosophical question over the nature and definition of renewal. Ford's "classes" do illustrate a possible tension within the prayer group-community movement. Renewalists seek two objectives: (1) spiritual renewal of the Catholic Church, (2) ecumenical outreach to the whole world. Communities which concentrate on the former may neglect the latter and vice-versa. The implicit problem is whether, given the exclusiveness of the Catholic Church, the inherently ecumenical nature of the covenant communities may contradict Catholic identity.

Renewalists attempt to neutralize this tension by a three-fold response: (1) they disavow any association with historical Catholic movements that were clearly deviant, (2) they identify with other well-known Catholic renewals such as the Biblical and Liturgical movements, and (3) an appeal is made to monasticism as an historical and philosophical precedent for the community movement.

Relative to the first, Ralph Martin maintains that renewalists are operating completely within the context of Catholicism and are not taking positions in any way contrary to the Church:

The one difference is that from the very beginning this renewal has planted itself firmly within the existing ecclesiastical authority and jurisdiction and has never claimed to be an independent source of discernment or guidance, but has always claimed to be under and submitted to the existing magisterium of the Church; and so, practically speaking, the Renewal's grown up everywhere in the Church.[42]

33

Verbal and even structural disassociation with
sectarian movements, however, does not negate the
possibility of affinities being present. Has not
every renewal movement made the same claim? Het-
erodoxy has always pleaded orthodoxy. Jansen up-
held no less a figure than St. Augustine against
the Jesuits;[43] Arius claimed to be the soul or
orthodoxy; the Fraticelle, the Brothers and Sisters
of The Free Spirit and the Apostolici all claimed
doctrinal and ecclesiastical purity.[44] Renewal
leaders also show a penchant for addressing difficult questions in terms of the general renewal
movement, ignoring the more controversial matter
of covenant communities.[45] Whether viewed as a
continnum or a dialectic, the existence of communities that are not Church-centered or exclusively
Catholic testifies against claims of ecclesiastical
propriety.

Association with modern and accepted
Catholic reforms is exemplified by Stephen Clark,
who associates Charismatic Renewal with the liturgical movement, CFM and the Cursillo as movements
that "have revitalized the life of the Church."[46]
Kevin Ranaghan observes that, "The liturgical movement was trying to strengthen a dimension of the
Church that is so fundamental that it is for all. . .
The same is true of the charismatic renewal."[47]

The argument against this defense is admir-
ably summarized by Catholic Sociologist Joseph
Fichter:

It does not behoove the social scientist
to indulge in forecasting, but it is possible
to point out dissimilarities between the organized cult of the Paraclete on the one hand
and the professional associations of scholars
and other experts that sponsored liturgical
reform and biblical studies on the other.
These "movements" never had induction ceremonies,
grass-roots membership, prayer households, diff-
erential service roles, levers of leadership
and authority, or a programmed and innovative
style of life. Unlike the Paraclete cult,
they were not institutionalized and organized

religious movements, and they did not com-
mand personal commitment.

The Catholic pentecostal movement may fade
in popularity, lose membership, and become dis-
organized, as has happened to some religious
congregations, but in sociological terms this
represents the death of failure rather than
obsorption into the "blood and life" of the
Church.[48]

Finally, there is the comparison of charismatic renewal with the ascetic tradition of Catholicism. The elements which constitute a covenant
community seem to be duplicated in monasticism.
The afore-mentioned elements of mysticism, male
authority and levels of leadership seem compatible
with covenant communities. Stephen Clark notes:

> Communities like the new charismatic com-
> munities have been common throughout the his-
> tory of the Church. As renewal movements
> have appeared and grown, the people involved
> have collected to form communities within the
> Church where they could live a life permeated
> by the movements' ideals--renewal communities.
> The ascetic movement produced the earliest
> monasteries and convents; the mendicant move-
> ment produced the great religious orders of
> Franciscans and Dominicans. Today, renewal
> communities are developing not only within
> the charismatic renewal, but also as part of
> the movement of communidades de base in the
> Latin countries of Europe and America. It
> seems to be almost a sociological law; renewal
> movements produce renewal communities.[49]

Since Catholic history has seen the
successful integration of many such movements, it
is argued that the Church possesses a "pastoral
wisdom of its own" which safeguards it against
sectarianism:

35

Catholicism has a pastoral wisdom of its own,
a wisdom nowhere more apparent than in an
ability to integrate renewal movements rather
than force them into separate sects. It has
had failures (perhaps its most notable failure
was the Protestant movement itself) and, to be
sure, there have been successes in Protestant
churches, but there is nonetheless an accum-
ulated wisdom belonging to the Catholic tradition which can easily be successful it applied
well. In fact, the much more orderly, constructive history of the Catholic charismatic renewal
in comparison to the earlier pentecostal movement and the more recent neo-pentecostal developments is in large part due to the instinctive
use of that wisdom by both the leaders of the
renewal and the hierarchy of the Church.[50]

This association seems by far the strongest
defense for the existence of covenant communities
within the Church. At the same time, however, it
is this comparison which most clearly displays the
spiritual, social and philosophical differences between such communities and normative Roman Catholicism.

First, there was a spiritual difference.
The early monastics were concerned with the ideal
Christian life. In <u>Life of St. Anthony</u>, Athanasius
urges that no sacrifice be spared in the quest for
virtue, for even if "the whole eighty years in the
religious life, or even a hundred, we shall not
reign for the life space of a hundred years, but
in return for the hundred we shall reign through
ages of ages."[51] Abbot St. Benedict writes,
. . . if we wish to dwell in the tabernacle of his
kingdom, except we run thither with good deeds we
shall not arrive."[52]

Anabaptists also created communities complete with authority figures and governmental
structure. There was, however, an important difference:

36

For the Anabaptist, the church was neither an institution (Catholicism), nor the instrument of God for the proclamation of the divine Word (Lutheranism), nor a resource group for individual piety (pietism). It was a brotherhood of love in which the fullness of the Christian life ideal is to be expected.[53]

The difference between covenant communities and historical monasticism is that the concept of "fellowship" or "brotherhood" never received a social identity which would in any way threaten ecclesiastical structures. The spiritual purpose of monasticism always preceded the social purpose. Because the monks had no children, they were free to pursue their theological motivations without assuming a sociological identity which would threaten the Church. Renewal communities, on the other hand, show greater affinity for anabaptistic ideals. A monastery is a soteriological statement; a community is a sociological environment.

The social dissimilarity calls attention to the question of whether the communities are properly cultic in character, or in reality are sectarian in nature. Communities will resist the sectarian label because they see themselves as religious cults that are both structurally and functionally contained within the larger Roman Catholic Church.[54]

Fichter notes that a "cult" in Roman Catholic theology means an "anamnesis", or a "recalling to mind" of some divine attribute or religious experience which is contained within the framework of the Church, but in need of greater emphasis and revival.[55] A "sect," on the other hand, would be a group of dissidents who separate from the parent church and "express defiance of the world or withdrawal from it."[56] On the basis of these definitions, Fichter concludes that Catholic pentecostalism represents authentic cultic renewal within the institutional Church;

The pentecostals are a group of Roman Catholics who associate for the purpose of intensifying their own spiritual life and of sharing with others the ecstatic experience of the gifts of the Holy Spirit. While the focus of this religious cult is God, the Paraclete, one may recall Becker's earlier description of the goal of the membership as "that of purely personal ecstatic experience, salvation, comfort, and mental or physical healing.[57]

Relative to covenant communities, Fichter states that, ". . .the great majority of them think of themselves as loyal members of the Church who have no intention of breaking off into a sectarian group."[58] Such communities are "not counter-ecclesial and only vaguely anti-institutional."[59] Because the purpose of the paraclete cult is to stress "interior renovation of the Spirit" as opposed to "institutional reform or adaptation", Fichter proceeds to label them as "an internal religious cult of renewal."[60]

While a cultic definition of Catholic charismatics in general is certainly permissible, one must question the extension of that cultic identity to covenant communities. Catholic definition of cult as anamnesis has a theological application as service expressly offered to God through sacred signs and inward dispositions which acknowledge God's supreme power--for example the veneration of saints.[61] By its very nature as an anamnesis, it is part of the Church or institution in which "memory" takes place. This would include monastic groups espousing devotion to particular saints. "Sect" comes from the Latin sequor, and means to specifically follow the doctrines and teachings of some religious, political or philosophical group.[62] It would be defined as a specifically "dissenting or schismatic religious body."[63]

By any common definition, however, the large covenant communities show every attribute of a sect.[64] The classical definitions of church and sect set forth by Ernst Troeltsch and developed

38

by later scholars would definitely place covenant communities in the latter category.[65]

Such monastic groups as the Cistercians, Francisicans and Dominicans conformed to the Church by becoming single organizations under a common rule.[66] They expanded and supported the ministry of the Church by widespread preaching and care of the parishes.[67] Within the Charismatic Renewal, such expansion is not taking place. What has been called "the first pentecostal Catholic parish" in Rockford, Ill. (The Community of the Holy Spirit) has disbanded after the priest became an Assembly of God minister.[68] Only one Catholic parish is said to have experienced renewal, and that is still uncertain.[69]

Further, although there are a number of charismatic priests, few are actually associated with the covenant communities. All that can be claimed is the general support of respective area bishops.[70] Kohler's statement that, "We are striving very hard to divest ourselves of institutional imagery," is indicative of an extremely sectarian attitude.[71] He also observes that, ". . . the way the Catholic Church is reaching people is pretty much useless. Its methods of outreach don't really say anything."[72] In every case where this author has hypothetically projected hierarchical censure concerning the charismatic experience, the persons questioned have expressed complete determination to persevere with the Renewal at any cost. Ford quotes Paul DeCelles, the Head Elder of People of Praise as saying, "I take issue with the notion that we should automatically obey a bishop who asks us to stop participation in the Catholic charismatic renewal."[73]

Sectarianism is further manifested in the pattern of authority within the communities. Outwardly, there again seems to be a parallel between monastery abbot and community elder. In the Rule for Monasteries, St. Benedict pictures the abbot

39

as directly answerable to God and responsible only
to the community-at-large.[74]   In covenant communities,
the elder or "chief-coordinator" is also answerable
only to God and the community-at-large.[75]

        In practice, however, there seems to be a
difference.   In the Rule of Benedict, the abbot
occupies a redemptive position similar to Christ.
He is specifically responsible for the salvation of
souls committed to him.[76] Such ministry functions
in complete harmony with ecclesiastical resources.
Proper confession is always available; duly or-
dained clergy are always present. Conversely, the
community elder seems to have more of an environ-
mental purpose. Stephen Clark defines the role of
an elder as follows:

        An environmental approach, then, is one
        that is concerned above all with the formation
        of environments or communities. The goal of
        an environmental approach is to get people to
        come together to interact in a personal way,
        to accept certain values, and not primarily
        to get something done.[77]

        Again, one senses a difference between
soteriology and sociology. Community members seem
to make little use of the confessional, being content to allow their immediate spiritual superiors
to handle all but the most grave sins.[78] Authority
in covenant communities seems to create a different
"atmosphere" than the same authority exercised in
a sacral institution. Timothy Stayton, a Lutheran
Benedictine monk, feels the Rule of the order is
often misapplied within covenant communities,
creating a feeling of severe Orwellian "presence"
rather than spiritual comfort and direction.[79]
The lack of sacral distinction seems to make the
primary purpose of the communities sociological.
The environmentalist seeks to build a community;
a "sacralist" sees the community already in existence within the parent institution, with his role
being that of approval or reform.[80]

Students of sectarian development such as
Richard Niebuhr and Liston Pope have observed that
the pressures of general society inevitably produce
a "denomination," that, "if the sect [cult] is defined rigorously, it cannot last beyond the founding
generation. Eventually, the sect [cult] will become a denomination [sect]."81 The monastic movement was able to turn in on itself, to return to
the Church, because it did not represent a social
unit conducive to this evolutionary pattern. Monastic forms were congruent with ecclesial molds;
communitarianism is not because its redemptive form
assumes a sociological pattern competitive to that
which gave it birth.

     The social nature of the community move-
ment at least partly explains the uniquely American
character of the charismatic renewal. Renewalists
feel that covenant communities are a specific answer
to the American problem of the nuclear family:

     The breakdown in urban neighborhoods in the
     United States since the end of World War II
     has had at least one fortunate effect. While
     the old closely-knit neighborhood had many
     advantages, it was perhaps a substitute for
     explicit Christian community. Its decline has
     helped us to realize that the life style of
     the nuclear family is totally inadequate to
     meet human and Christian needs and that ten-
     dencies toward isolated individualism result
     in the further fragmentation of an environment
     of alienation. Thus, the Spirit, who always
     draws the members of the Body of Christ to-
     gether, has shown us once more that Christian
     life is essentially meant to be communal.
     These basic Christian communities draw heavily
     on St. Paul's analogy of church life to a
     living organism. For me, this is a revelation
     from the Lord concerning his plan for future
     Christian living. I have no difficulty fore-
     seeing, in faith, the future universal church
     composed of such communities.82

Interestingly, renewal by extended communities continues to be symptomatic church life
in the United States. A community has recently
been started in Brussels, Belgium through the
transfer of several Renewal leaders and their
families from South Bend.[83] This society, however, is as technologically advanced as the United
States. For Catholics, renewal by ecumenical
covenant communities remains a particularly American phenomenon.

The validity of such structures for Catholicism is extremely doubtful. When the sociological pressures of a nuclear society are eased
by the presence and ministry of charismatic
leaders, a society within a society is born. A
society thus created, that is not specifically
scral and extends past the first generation, will
of necessity assume a sectarian posture.

Finally, there exists an implicit philosophical difference between monasticism and
covenant communities. A monastic world-view
may be described as a "heteronomy," in which reality is viewed as a hierarchy with the sacred
reigning over the profane.[84] The Protestant re-
formers, denying such a division between the sacred
and the secular, did away with monasteries, allow-
ing no religious order as such until the appearance
of deaconesses during the nineteenth century.[85]

Communities, however, illustrate an
ontonomy--a world-view which stresses the universe
as a unity.[86] An excellent example is Benjamin
Zablocki's study of the Bruderhof entitled, The
Joyful Community. Zablocki's thesis, highly popular with Catholic charismatics, is the complete
denial of any secular sphere of life. He even
goes so far as to compare the Bruderhof with a
Zen monastery. The primary concern of the community is to bear witness in the simple, everyday
acts of living. Sacraments and rituals are de-
emphasized and there is not even a church building.[87]

42

The Zen Buddhist monastery operates in the same manner. All activities are of equal importance; "Nothing is preparation for anything else. . . Everything is what it is."[88] Thus, Zablocki concludes:

> The Bruderhof and the Zen monastery have quite different purposes. What they have in common is a desire to destroy the notion of a secular sphere of life. The message is that there are no activities, however trivial, that cannot be permeated by the divine spirit.[89]

The implicit point of contradiction between Catholic monasticism and modern communitarians is thus vague but critical: monastics attempted to reign over the secular; communitarians seek its destruction. To them, there can be no notion of a secular sphere of life. Such "unitheism" logically deprives the Church of a separate existence. One is led to the self-contradiction of communities attempting to fulfill both institutional and ecumenical objectives. Such a process can only militate against the best interests of Catholicism. It is impossible for the communities to "be assimilated into the life-blood of the Church," to "disappear," as long as their blantantly ecumenical structure poses a contradiction to the exclusivity of the Church.

It is reasonable to suppose that the covenant communities will evolve in the same manner as the Bruderhof. The same elements--charismatic leadership, subsequent generations and an ontonomical world-view--should produce the same result. Consequently, one may predict a twofold destiny for renewal communities. Those undefined, informal, ecclesiastically-oriented or led groups pose no threat to the Church and will continue to make their own unique spiritual contributions. The larger, highly-structured and ecumenical covenant communities, however, do pose a threat to the Church and will either be sanctioned or subjected to severe clerical authority in the near future.

Perhaps the exact reason for this can be most clearly seen in the incompatibility of the communities' own objectives with their basic identity. Through assuming the necessary form in minister, they invariably adopt the mold of the institution which has given them birth. They become a visible portrayal of the spiritual relationship between God and man. When this happens, they become ensnared in the dilemma framed so well by Karl Barth:

> For is there any relationship of man with man whose structure may try to imitate that between God and man institutionally? Is there any authority of man which can represent to other men the authority of God institutionally? Is there a real obedience, not of works only, but of the heart which men can feel bound to render to other men institutionally? In a relationship between sinful men will not this necessarily mean that the majesty of God is obscured, that a burden is laid upon both those who have to command and those who have to obey, which neither can bear? Will not the attempt to actualize institutionally, a representation of the communio sanctorum, inevitably result in an illusion which does injury to God and falsely exalts one man and falsely debases another?[90]

The Catholic answer to this question lies in the very institution Barth was attacking--the visible and sacral body of Christ. This body is at once both archetype and ectype. By definition, its pattern is exclusive and its authority final. Only in the Church can the Sacred truly be ascertained through reference to the logical categories of the Holy. Any group which purports to portray the relationship of man to God visible violates the distinction of the Church as a revelational and sacramental "given" and is therefore heretical and divisive.

NOTES

1. Joseph H. Fichter, The Catholic Cult of the
   Paraclete. (New York: Sheed & Ward, 1975),
   p. 32.
2. Whitney Smith, "Charismatics: United or Hell-
   Bent for Schism," South Bend Tribune. July 7, 1977.
3. Fichter, Catholic Cult. p. 31.
4. Ibid., p. 32.
5. Kerry Kohler, Telephone Interview, Nov. 16, 1977.
6. Bertil W. Ghezzi, "Three Charismatic Communities,"
   As the Spirit Leads Us. Kevin and Dorothy
   Ranaghan, eds. (New York: Paulist Press, 1971),
   p. 167.
7. Ibid., pp. 167-183.
8. Kerry Kohler Interview, Nov. 16, 1977.
9. David Hulen, "Charismatic Drive Big Business,"
   South Bend Tribune. Aug. 7, 1977.
10. Ford, Which Way for Catholic Pentecostals?, p. 3.
11. Jill Whitney, "Facts for the Press," The 1976
    Continental Conference of the Charismatic Renewal
    in the Catholic Church. University of Notre
    Dame, May 28-30, 1975.
12. International Directory of Catholic Charismatic
    Prayer Groups. (South Bend, Ind.: Charismatic
    Renewal Services, 1975-76), p. 163.
13. Fichter, Catholic Cult. p. 58.
14. Kevin Ranaghan, Catholic Pentecostals. (New York:
    Paulist Press, 1969), p. 234.
15. Bob Bell, "Charismatic Communities: Questions
    and Cautions," New Covenant, July, 1973, p. 4.
16. Ghezzi, "Three Charismatic Communities," p. 166.
17. Ibid., p. 186.
18. Stephen B. Clark, "Charismatic Renewal in the
    Church," As The Spirit Leads Us. p. 33.
19. Kerry Kohler, Private Interview, South Bend,
    Ind., Oct. 16, 1977.
20. Kerry Kohler, Telephone Interview, Valparaiso,
    Ind., Nov. 16, 1977.
21. James Robbins, Personal Interview, South Bend,
    Ind., May 29, 1976.
22. "Covenant Communities--What's Happening in the
    Renewal Today," 1976 Continental Conference on
    the Charismatic Renewal in the Catholic Church.
    Press Conference, May 29, 1976, South Bend, Ind.

23. Kohler Interview, Nov. 16, 1977.
24. George Martin, Parish Renewal: A Charismatic Approach. (Ann Arbor, Mich.: Word of Life, 1976), p. 60.
25. Ford, Which Way for Catholic Pentecostals?. pp. 1-4.
26. Ibid., pp. 4, 61.
27. Ibid., p. 1.
28. Ibid., p. 61.
29. Ibid., p. 1.
30. Ibid., p. 65.
31. Ibid., p. 1.
32. Ibid., p. 68.
33. Ibid., p. 69.
34. Ralph Martin, Private Interview, 1976 Continental Conference on the Charismatic Renewal. South Bend, Ind., May 29, 1976.
35. Ford, Which Way for Catholic Pentecostals?, p. 5.
36. Ibid., p. 13.
37. Ibid., p. 18.
38. Ibid., pp. 11-12.
39. St. Athanasius, "Life of St. Anthony," Readings in Church History, ed. Colman J. Barry, 1 vol. (Westminster, Md.: The Newman Press, 1965), 1:155-59.
40. Abbot John Cassian, "Conference IX on Prayer," Readings in Church History. 1:162-63.
41. Abbot St. Benedict, "Rule of Monasteries," Readings in Church History. 1:169-70.
42. Martin Interview, May 29, 1976, South Bend, Ind.
43. Kenneth Scott Latourette, A History of Christianity. (New York: Harper & Row, 1953), p. 877.
44. New Catholic Encyclopedia, "History of Heresy," 1:1064-65.
45. The more ecclesiastically authoritative writings of the Renewal ignore the community aspect. Theological and Pastoral Initiations. (Notre Dame, Ind.: Word of Life, 1974), a committee document chaired by Cardinal Suenens, the most influential papal supporter of the movement, makes no mention of the communities. Cardinal Suenen's own book, A New Pentecost? (New York: Seabury Press, 1975), makes only passing mention of them.

46. Stephen B. Clark, Building Christian Communities. (Notre Dame, Ind.: Ave Maria Press, 1972, p. 158.
47. Kevin Ranaghan, "Charismatic Renewal in the Church," As The Spirit Leads Us. p. 27.
48. Fichter, Catholic Cult. p. 38.
49. Stephen B. Clark, Unordained Elders and Renewal Communities. (New York: Paulist Press, 1976), p. 4.
50. Ibid., p. 2.
51. Barry, Readings in Church History. p. 155.
52. Ibid., p. 167.
53. Ford, Which Way for Catholic Pentecostals?, p. 53.
54. Fichter, Catholic Cult of the Paraclete. pp. 19-20.
55. Ibid., pp. 20-21.
56. Ibid., pp. 21-22.
57. Ibid., p. 23.
58. Ibid., p. 31.
59. Ibid.
60. Ibid., p. 32.
61. Karl Rahner and Herbert Vorgrimler, Theological Dictionary. Cornelius Ernst, ed., and Richard Strachan, trans (New York: Herder & Herder, 1965), p. 112.
62. New Catholic Encyclopedia. 13:31.
63. Webster's Seventh New Collegiate Dictionary. (Springfield, Mass.: G & C Merriam Co., 1965), p. 780.
64. A sociologist may use the word "denomination" for the theological equivalent of "sect." Also, the terms "sect" and "cult" may at times be interchangeable with the theological concept of a "cult." Finally, the sociologist views the cult-sect labels as a continuum; the latter is always in the process of "becoming" from the former. A theologian, dealing with sacral institutions, does not necessarily view the terms as process.
65. The Church has the following significant attributes:
    1. Membership in fact upon the basis of birth
    2. Administration of the formalized means of grace and their sociological and theological concomitants--hierarchy and dogma
    3. Inclusiveness of social structure, often coinciding with geographical or ethnic boundaries

47

The <u>Sect</u> is characterized by:
1. Separatism from the general society, and withdrawal from or defiance of the world and its institutions and values
2. Exclusiveness both in attitude and in social structure
3. Emphasis upon a conversion experience prior to membership
4. Voluntary joining
5. A spirit of regeneration
6. An attitude of ethical austerity, often of an ascetic nature

Source: <u>The Sociology of Religion</u>. Thomas F. O'dea (Englewood Cliffs, N.J.: Prentice-Hall, 1966), p. 68.
66. Latourette, <u>A History of Christianity</u>. p. 569.
67. Ibid.
68. Kohler Interview, Nov. 20, 1977.
69. Ibid.
70. Ibid.
71. Ibid.
72. Ibid.
73. Ford, <u>Which Way for Catholic Pentecostals</u>?. p. 49.
74. Barry, <u>Readings in Church History</u>. p. 170.
75. Interview statement by Kohler: "Everyone is under authority; I share my personal decisions or problems with the brother who is over me."

Question: Who is over your? Answer: Kevin Ranaghan.
Question: Who is over Kevin Ranaghan? Answer: Paul Decelles.
Question: Who is over Paul DeCelles? Answer: Well, it gets sort of tricky here. We've received a lot of criticism over the concept of internal authority. Technically, Paul DeCelles is responsible to the community-at-large. It turns back in on itself.
Question: Is there a priest over DeCelles? Answer: No.
Question: Are priests generally associated with the communities?
Answer: No. We are trying to de-emphasize the denominational distinctives as much as possible. Our philosophy is to prepare lay brothers to

take vows in whatever church they represent.
(Oct. 16, 1977, South Bend, Ind.)

76. Barry, Readings in Church History. p. 170.
77. Clark, Building Christian Communities. p. 121.
78. Kohler Interview, Oct. 16, 1977.
79. Private Interview, Timothy Stayton, Valparaiso
    University, Valparaiso, Ind., Feb. 2, 1978.
80. Thomas F. O'Dea, The Sociology of Religion.
    (Englewood Cliffs, N.J.: Prentice-Hall, 1966),
    p. 69.
81. Ibid.
82. Kevin Ranaghan, The Lord, The Spirit and the
    Church. (Notre Dame, Ind.: Charismatic Renew-
    al Services, 1973), pp. 38-39.
83. Kathleen Harsh, "Charismatics Live Together,"
    South Bend Tribune. South Bend, Ind., Aug. 7,
    1977, p. 30.
84. George Hoyer, "Preaching the Types of Salvation
    History to Secularized Christians," The 1978
    Institute of Liturgical Studies. Valparaiso
    University, Valparaiso, Ind., Feb. 2, 1978.
85. William Anthone Cleobsch, "Communities and
    Orders: Protestant," Twentieth Century Ency-
    clopedia of Religious Knowledge. (Grand Rapids,
    Mich.: Baker Book House, 1955) 1:278.
86. Hoyer, Valparaiso University, Feb. 2, 1978.
87. Benjamin Zablocki, The Joyful Community.
    (Baltimore, Md.: Penguin Books, 1971), p. 31.
88. Ibid.
89. Ibid.
90. E.J. Tinsley, "Monasticism," A Dictionary of
    Christian Theology. Alan Richardson, ed.
    (Philadelphia: Westminster Press, 1969), p. 222.

CHAPTER IV

CHARISMATIC RENEWAL AND THE CHURCH

The charismatic renewal has much more
official support than casual observers might realize.
This is so for two reasons: (1) the influence of
Léon Joseph Cardinal Suenens, the influential figure
of Vatican II who is the highest ranking ecclesiastical personality involved in the renewal, and
(2) the official posture of the epochal Lumen
Gentium, asserted by Pope Paul VI to be "the principle object of attention of the Second Vatican
Ecumenical Council."[1]

Léon Joseph Cardinal Suenens, Archbishop
of Malines-Bruxelles (Belgium) first appeared on
the charismatic renewal scene at the 1973 International Conference held at Notre Dame, Indiana.[2]
Since then, he has been a dominent figure. His
A New Pentecost?, an apologetic for the charismatic
renewal, was spoken of by Pope Paul VI as a val-
uable treatment of renewal in which, "The abundant
outpouring of supernatural graces, which are called
charisms, can truly mark a providential hour in
the history of the Church."[3] He is responsible
for formally introducing the renewal to Europe by
transplanting several renewal leaders and their
families from South Bend, Indiana to Brussels for
the purpose of establishing renewal communities
in Belgium.[4]

What is not as widely known is that the
same Cardinal Suenens was and is a primary figure
in the formulation of Catholic policy. He has
been widely acclaimed as the principal proponent
of structural reforms--of "reorganizing the Church
from the Roman Curia down to the local parish."[5]
At Vatican II he was one of four members of a new
governing body of four moderators appointed by
Pope Paul VI to provide a theological identity
for the Council:

51

This group of moderators was now expected to provide effective direction and also to give the Council a particular theological identity. The choice of persons was itself significant. At least Cardinals Lercaro, Suenens and Dopfner had unequivocally declared their theological views during the first session. By nominating them, the pope himself had preset the Council's theological mold. In their choice he had also shown by repeated expressions of sympathy for the Cardinal from Belgium.[6]

The purpose of this group (with the death of Paul VI, Suenens remains the only living member) was to state and amplify the Pope's own formulation of a four-point program for the Council.

The first task of the Council was to deal with the Church's interpretation of its own nature . . . the second. . . was the renewal of the Church, the third the reestablishment of unity among Christians, and the fourth the Church's dialogue with contemporary man.[7]

Relative to the Church's interpretation of its own nature, the Pope projected a sketch which envisioned the coming of the Spirit to Christ's disciples at Pentecost as an "antetype" of the Church. "Thus Christological and Spirit-centered elements were given preeminence. . . in the definition of the Church."[8]

The Council responded by producing a document of five chapters dealing successively with the mystery of the Church, the Church as the People of God, the hierarchical structure of the Church, the laity, and the holiness of the Church. This new text (other chapters were added later) was mainly the work of the Belgian theologians of Cardinal Suenens' circle, "It reflected their position, midway between Roman and Spanish scholasticism and the boldly modern writings of German and French theologians."[9]

This document is most significant in that it emphasizes the evolution of Rome's own definition of itself as the body of Christ. With Vatican II, the visible, physical body of Bellarmine, having evolved to the visible social body of Pius XIII, became finally the charismatic body of Paul VI:

By contrast, with Bellarmine and Pius XII the new text returned wholeheartedly to the total biblical testimony about the Church. Here the idea of the "body of Christ" is complemented with that of the "People of God." Here the Church is seen as determined by pneumatological as well as christological elements; the Church is charismatic as well as sacramental in structure. In short, the idea of the Church evidences the full biblical polarity.[10]

The background of this text witnessed a full-fledged debate between the progressive Suenens and conservative Cardinal Ruffini. The latter urged that charisms be relegated to the past and warned that any overemphasis on charismatic religious experience would endanger the institutional Church.[11] Suenens, in his Vatican II speech, "The Charismatic Dimension of the Church," contended for a more charismatic dimension of the Church to be developed in the whole chapter (referring specifically to chapter II), a greater emphasis on the importance of charisms in the people of God and a more "positive and constructive" statement of the relation of pastors to charisms of the faithful.[12]

Although Suenens is by far the most powerful ecclesiastic behind the renewal, other clerical support is not lacking. Ralph Martin observes that:

. . . the most remarkable feature of this third stream of the pentecostal movement is the encouragement and active support charismatic Catholics have received from the highest levels of church leadership. As of this writing 1975 , I am personally aware of approximately twenty bishops in eleven different countries who are personally involved in the renewal, including Cardinal Suenens of Belgium, and more than forty others who are very close to personal involvement. In October 1973, Pope Paul received thirteen Catholic charismatic leaders in a special audience to express his genuine appreciation and encouragement of the renewal. On October 16, 1974, he stated in a public audience that the Church can have a new abundance of charismatic gifts and that the event of Pentecost must continue in the Church and in the world. The Pope specifically recommended Cardinal Suenens' book A New Pentecost?, in that address; the book examines the outpouring of the Holy Spirit in the Church with special reference to the charismatic renewal.[13]

Mention must also be made of the potential relationship with the new Pope, John Paul II, who will likely have a positive attitude toward the renewal. Although he is known as a theological conservative, much of his support came from Americans and a nucleus of liberal Europeans who were impressed by his commitment to Vatican II reforms.[14] Indeed, the greatest resistance to his election came from ultraconservatives.[15]

Culturally, his old-world Catholic background is less secularized than that of the West. As a youth the Pope was attracted to the writings of St. John of the Cross, Spain's 16th century Carmelite mystic.[16] Like Luther, his entrance into the priesthood was preceded by the death of a loved one (his father) in 1941.[17]

Ecclesiastically, the Pope displays an aptitude for innovation and an acceptance of spiritual enterprises which would at one time

54

have been unthinkable to Catholicism. He personally invited Billy Graham to preach at St. Anne's
Church in Cracow, an event that took place just
four days before his election as Pope.[18] He is
also friendly to an evangelical youth-oriented
movement called Oasis which has connections with
both Catholic charismatics and Protestant evan-
gelicals.[19] Franscisvek Blachnicki, the director
of the movement, recently spent two weeks at
Campus Crusade for Christ headquarters in California.[20] An Oasis rally in the summer of 1978
attracted 27,000 people.[21]

        Intellectually, Pope John Paul II is an
expert in phenomenology, which in an odd manner
seems very accommodating to charismatic thought-
patterns.[22] Basically, charismatic religious experience seems to be an appeal to empirical verification of that experience. One could well argue
that charismatics are actually phenomenalists.

        The content of Cardinal Wojytla's own
religious experience reflected a view of laity
and sense of evangelical purpose identical to
renewal objectives. In his commentary on the
Vatican II "Decree on the Apostolate of the Laity",
he stresses the value of the text in emphasis upon a personal sense of the apostolate.[23] This
same document contains the most supportive and
specific statement concerning charismatic gifts
to be found in the Documents.

        Relative to religious life, the Pope pro-
jects an evangelical spiritual inwardness as
opposed to political and social outwardness. Said
to be the author of article forty-six of De Ecclesia,[24]
he maintains that, "Christ should be shown contemplating on the mountain, announcing God's kingdom to the multitude, healing the sick and the
maimed, turning sinners to wholesome fruit,
blessing children, doing good to all, and always
obeying the will of the Father who sent Him."[25]

During a recent audience with Cardinal Suenens, Pope John Paul II confirmed and renewed the mandate given to Suenens by Paul VI--to guide "the evolution of the Catholic charismatic movement so that it enters fully into the Church."[26] The Pope also expressed his appreciation for the Second Malines Document on ecumenism and indicated his desire for Suenens to continue in the charismatic effort.[27]

Finally, Wojytla's election may enhance the position of the charismatic renewal in that it disassociates papal primacy from the geography of Rome, thus weakening any Vatican bureaucracy which would seek to limit or oppose the movement.

Relative to the theological position of Vatican II documents, one must recognize that Lumen Gentium represents a genuine innovation in Catholic thought concerning the spiritual element in the Church. Before the Second Vatican Council, the most significant "preparation" for the renewal was the encyclical letter, On the Holy Spirit, published by Pope Leo XIII in 1897.[28] This letter consists of a routine summary, "precise and authoritative but not otherwise remarkable, of Catholic teaching about the Holy Spirit."[29] The most significant contribution of the letter seems to be the definition of Spirit indwelling Church in the Western sense of soul indwelling body:

> Let it suffice to state that as Christ is the Head of the Church, so is the Holy Ghost her soul. "What the soul is in our body, that is the Holy Ghost in Christ's body, the the Church." This being so, no further and fuller "manifestation and revelation of the divine "Spirit" may be imagined or expected; for that which now takes place in the Church is the most perfect possible, and will last until that day when the Church herself, having passed through her militant career, shall be taken up into the joy of the saints triumphing in heaven.[30]

While _Divinium_ _Illud_ represents the only
encyclical support for charismatic renewal prior
to Vatican II, Edward O'Connor notes at least three
independent but complementary theological developments which further paved the way for renewal.
These were: (1) Johann Adam Moehler's ideas on
the place of the Holy Spirit in the Church, (2) the
emphasis of Matthias Scheeben (1835-1888) on the
work of the Spirit in the individual Christian and,
(3) the gradual rediscovery by historians of the
role of charismata in the early Church.[31]

In addition to these, one may note at
least four sociological-theological movements
which made the general Catholic populace more conscious of the Holy Spirit:

The liturgical movement, the biblical movement,
the ecumenical movement, and what might be
called the movement for rehabilitation of the
laity, converged to bring about a lively new
consciousness of the mystery of the Church.
This, perhaps the most significant development in the Catholic mentality during the
first half of the twentieth century, tended
to foster a greater awareness of the role of
the Holy Spirit. Moreover, in various ways,
these four movements prepared people directly
for some of the particular fruits that were
to arise out of the charismatic renewal.[32]

Thus, by the time of Vatican II, the
Catholic religious climate was favorable to a more
official stance on charisms and the place of the
Holy Spirit within the Church. The _Constitution_
_on_ _the_ _Church_ accomplishes this purpose by clearly
stating the charismatic nature of the Church in a
manner which renewalists feel strongly supports
their position.

First, _De_ _Ecclesia_ in chapter one ("The
Mystery of the Church") incorporates into its language the major historical views concerning the

nature of the Church. The body of Christ is spoken
of as "a kind of sacrament," a "mystery" present
when all believers break eucharistic bread. The
relationship between the Spirit and the Church is
described in terms of "indwelling in a temple,"
in the time-honored Western sense of furnishing,
directing and endowing.[33] The institutional Church
of Bellarmine is present by definition as a governed
society; the visible and mystical church of Pius
XII and Leo XIII is presented as a visible community of faith in which, "the society furnished with
hierarchical agencies and the Mystical Body of
Christ are not to be considered as two realities."[34]

The innovation of the chapter, however, is
that while preserving familiar terminology, it at
the same time changes the concept of the Church to
a more charismatic viewpoint. Whereas Pius XII
identified without qualification the mystical body
of Christ with the Catholic Church in a manner
which interpreted "body" as "body social," the Constitution identifies mystical body as communion of
life with Christ.[35] The Church in her earthly
pilgrimage is seen first and foremost as the spiritual fellowship of her baptized members, and only
secondarily, and as it were consequentially, as a
hierarchized communion.[36] Such a position constitutes a direct contradiction of the thesis of Pius
XII:

. . .the society furnished with hierarchical
agencies and the Mystical Body of Christ . . .
form one interlocked reality which is comprised
of a divine and a human element . . . This
Church, constituted and organized in the world
as a society, subsists in italics mine the
Catholic Church, which is governed by the successor of Peter and by the bishops in union with
that successor, although many elements of sanctification and of truth can be found outside of
her visible structure.[37]

Another point of accommodation is the
Constitution's treatment of non-Catholic Christians
and their communions. Although vague and "curiously
untheological," the document remains always friendly

and hopeful of future rapprochement.[38] For the
first time in Catholic conciliar history, Protestants are recognized as true Churches! Such
feelings are extremely compatible with the charismatic concept of Church as "presence" which transcends both history and dogma.

Second, the Council in chapter II emphasized
the human and communal side of the Church as "The
People of God" in a manner supportive of the charismatic renewal. This chapter, directly inserted by
Cardinal Suenens,[39] provides some of the most
beautiful language in the Constitution. The Church
is spoken of as "the new Israel according to the
Spirit," who, through Christ, "has a heritage of
dignity and freedom as the sons of God, in whose
hearts the Holy Spirit dwells as in His temple."[40]
The Church as the People of God (referring to the
total community of pastors and faithful) transcends
all limits of time and race and moving forward
through trial and tribulation maintains her fidelity
to her Lord; "that moved by the Holy Spirit she
may never cease to renew herself, until through the
cross she arrives at the light which knows no
setting."[41]

The very language of the chapter, in com-
menting on such Scriptures as Jer. 31:31-34,
I Cor. 11:25, I Pet. 1:23 and John 3:5-6, lends
itself to charismatic emphasis and thought-patterns.
The Spirit dwells in individual hearts as in His
temple; the baptized are made a spiritual house and
holy priesthood through regeneration and the anoint-
ing of the Holy Spirit.[42]

Finally, the emphasis of chapter II in
the calling of all to be the new People of God reflects an incipient denial of the old exclusiveness. This complements the broad, less doctrinally
clear religious experience common to charismatics.

All men are called to be part of this
catholic unity of the People of God, a unity
which is harbinger of the universal peace it

promotes. And there belong to it or are re-
lated to it in various ways, the Catholic
faithful as well as all who believe in Christ,
and indeed the whole of mankind. For all men
are called to salvation by the grace of God.[43]

With reference to Orthodox and other separated
brethren:

The Church recognizes that in many ways
she is linked with those who, being baptized
are honored with the name of Christian, though
they do not profess the faith in its entirety
or do not preserve unity of communion with the
successor of Peter.[44]

Even those who dwell in "shadows and images," the
non-Christian religious, may "attain to ever-
lasting salvation" by sincerely following the dic-
tates of their conscience.[45] Such emphasis on
subjective experience seems parallel to charismatic religious experience.

Based on these texts, it is quite evident
why charismatic renewal leaders feel this is their
time. In the words of Cardinal Suenens:

The long history of the Church is filled with
the wonders of the Holy Spirit.
Think only of the prophets and saints who, in
times of darkness, have discovered a spring
of grace and shed beams of light on our path.
I believe in the surprises of the Holy Spirit.
John XXIII came as a surprise, and the Council,
too.
They were the last things we expected.
Who would dare say that the love and imagination
of God were exhausted?[46]

At this point two criticisms should be made.
First, the stress on spiritual commonality and consequent lessening of the Roman claim of exclusiveness seems to lead Catholicism in the direction of
universalism. The question is whether any meaningful type of theological identity can therefore be

maintained. Since the charismatic experience lends itself to such a framework, the Church will have to guard against any compromise of its theological identity. This problem will be more fully developed in the chapter on ecumenism.

Second, there seems to be a basic difference in goals between Vatican II and the charismatic renewal. Renewal to the Catholic Church means aggiornamento, the updating of method or the way in which theology is presented to the modern world. Cullman notes the dual task of aggiornamento as adaptation of the form of the gospel to the modern world and discussion with the world so that, ". . . every era must formulate the old confession and discuss theology with the contemporary world."[47] Joseph Fichter notes that:

> . . . much of the emphasis has been on organizational and structural problems: the revamping of the Vatican Curia, the establishment of episcopal synods, pastoral councils and associations or clergy and religious women, and the encouragement of co-responsibility and co-llegiality in the affairs of the Church.[48]

The thrust of this idea is a complete change from the massive apologetical and theological structures of the seventeenth and eighteenth centuries to a "theology and apologetic of the future" which may assume any form.[49] David Wells notes that the Church even went so far as to use the word reformatio to describe its goal.[50]

Logically, this would seem to be a milieu of unlimited potential for the charismatic renewal. But one has to remember that the Church always speaks from a conceptual position of total authority. The concept here is that of communicating the purity of truth already in one's possession. "If we can make ourselves understood-- if we can modernize--." This posture leads to a "speaking down" or a "speaking out" which seems somehow to bypass the personal in favor of the institutional.

Charismatic renewalists, on the other hand, speak in terms that are revivalistic and personal. A spiritual message is spoken to the interior of the Church--perhaps one could speak of the Church talking to itself. But what could be the source of such a message? Who, or what can speak to the Church inwardly? Catholicism requires as one of its prime ingredients an ecclesiastical relationship. Relationship with God is not primarily individualistic or personal in the subjective sense, but rather is made personally real by "passing through a Church framework that is definitely public, comprising an established ministry, sacraments, etc."51 Yves Congar makes an apt observation:

Unless I am mistaken, this is where the line of division between the Protestant Reformation and the ancient Church should be drawn. The Reformation wished to react against a development that was sometimes excessive and often mingled with impure and questionable elements, arising from human and fallible interventions. It rejected them and broke free, but omitted to distinguish between the historical accretions which needed reforming, and the divine institution, which should have been respected as such. It replaces a religious relationship that was intrinsically ecclesiastical by one in which the basic elements constituting it were of a purely personal nature; a certain communal note was added subsequently, but it was more of an external addition than an integral part. Each individual formed his own religious relationship by faith, in reply to the Word of God, attained by a personal contact with the Bible.52

This is the same conflict which faces the charismatic renewal. Only the Church may interpret the Church. The self-understanding of Catholicism holds that she is not just another church,

to be evaluated by other individuals or churches
or groups:

> Even after the most positive evaluation of the
> Spirit at work in the other churches, even
> while recognizing that they are positive instru-
> ments of salvation, Vatican II declared: "It
> is through Christ's Catholic Church alone,
> which is the universal help towards salvation,
> that the fullness of the means of salvation can
> be obtained.[53]

The Church is therefore self-authenticating, with
the magisterium being the only criterion for the
content of religious experience. Objective
ecclesiastical experience always has priority over
subjective charismatic experience.

After all has been said, Rome must resist
denominational reductionism. Aggiornamento cannot
usurp Catholic essence. Renewal must always conform to a posture of obedience and humility before
visible authority and finality. The Church brings
salvation, the Church beings revelation, therefore
only the Church can renew the Church. This is
why Catholic reforms have been primarily institutional in nature. A renewal based on subjective
experience cannot renew the Church any more than
another church could renew the Church. Through
the Church the Holy Spirit speaks. For the Church
to maintain its position of authority there is a
sense in which the Church must precede the Spirit.
The charismatic renewal, by listening to voices
that are interior and experential, seeks a renewal
basically foreign to the essence of Catholicism.
How can one renew invisibly and interiorly that
which is constituted authoritative by the very
fact of its visibility?

This tension between subjectivism and
objective ecclesiology is further demonstrated in
renewalist eschatology. Charismatic leaders make
much of Karl Rahner's baleful vision of Christians
becoming a "diaspora" of individuals and groups

practicing faith in "an otherwise secularized, if not paganized, world."[54] They maintain that the charismatic is the Holy Spirit bringing about the renewal sought by Vatican II through personalized experience.[55] The future of the charismatic renewal is a "charismatically renewed Church" which will bring the day when "our popes and bishops perform miracles, as we pray for them to do when they are consecrated, or when they are guided by prophecies and visions, as popes and bishops have been in times past."[56] Further, in a charismatically renewed Church:

> . . . the choice of persons for roles of pastoral leadership (e.g., pastors, bishops, popes) would be made solely on the basis of the Spirit that would equip him for such a role. Thus, however and by whomever the choice was made, ultimately it would be the Holy Spirit himself who, by the distribution of his gifts, would designate the leaders for the Church.[57]

In such a framework the Spirit is given a role which seems to violate his historical place in the Church. In the words of Congar, "The New Testament texts are so positive that we cannot do better than to summarize them in the traditional expression describing the Holy Ghost as 'the soul of the Church'."[58] The renewal seems to violate this principle so that the Spirit assumes a relation to the Church outside its normal function. Catholicism sees a complete integration of physical, visible and spiritual elements so that the unity of Church and Spirit is indeed like the unity of body and soul, a "besouled body," rather than an extrapolated dichotomy. In seeking the authority of the Spirit, renewalists seem to produce a needless tension between these two elements.

Renewal leaders seem to be making the understandable Hegelian error of viewing themselves as an ultimate historical synthesis which will serve as a sina qua non for the Church of tomorrow. A more realistic assessment is provided by Karl Rahner:

If you'll get the history of the Church,
there's always these renewal movements, e.g.,
the monks, the Franciscans, the sixteenth
century Jesuits; these always at the moment
tend to over-value themselves; they see themselves as the renewal of the Church, but if
you look at the Franciscans, how they looked
upon themselves as the "new light" or the
"final reform" of the Church, but in time you
see how it was limited, how it had a certain
very useful, good effect but nevertheless
very limited; or the Jesuits in their work in
the Counter-Reformation--there was a positive
thing but nevertheless there were all sorts of
other things going on, so at the moment there's
this tendency to over-value for the Church the
importance of the movement, but in time one
can see its limitations.[59]

The charismatic renewal will be assisted,
even strengthened through ecclesiastical sponsor-
ship and the compatibility of its language and
goals with the stated language and goals of Vatican
II. At the core of the movement, however, a
different voice seems to be directing. This voice
is called the Holy Spirit--but it is the Spirit
speaking outside the magisterium. The Spirit in
the charismatic renewal seems to assume a different
relationship or posture toward the Church which
limits and even demotes the institution. Given
the Roman position on authority and exclusiveness,
one wonders how far the renewal can go before a
reconstruction becomes necessary.

NOTES

1. The Documents of Vatican II. Walter M. Abbott, gen. ed., and Joseph Gallagher, trans. ed. (New York: Guild Press, 1966), p. 10.
2. Ralph Martin, "About This Issue," New Covenant. July, 1973, p. 2.
3. Léon Joseph Suenens, A New Pentecost? (New York: Seabury Press, 1975), flyleaf.
4. Harsh, "Charismatics Live Together," South Bend Tribune. Aug. 7, 1977, p. 30.
5. Fichter, Catholic Cult. p. 4.
6. Joseph Ratzinger, Theological Highlights of Vatican II. (New York: Paulist Press, 1966), p. 37.
7. Ibid., pp. 41-42.
8. Ibid., p. 41.
9. Ibid., p. 44.
10. Ibid., p. 49.
11. Suenens, A New Pentecost?. p. 30.
12. Léon Joseph Suenens, "The Charismatic Dimension of the Church," Council Speeches of Vatican II. Han Küng, Yves Congar and Daniel O'Hanlon, eds. (New York: Paulist Press, 1964), p. 34.
13. Ralph Martin, Fire on the Earth. (Ann Arbor, Mich.: Word of Life, 1975), pp. 34-35.
14. Gregory Wierzynski, "A Foreign Pope," Time. October 30, 1978, p. 87.
15. Ibid.
16. Ibid., p. 93.
17. Ibid.
18. Ibid., p. 97.
19. Robert D. Lindner and Richard V. Pierard, "Poland Opens the Door to Billy Graham," Christianity Today. Oct. 6, 1978, pp. 44-45.
20. Ibid., p. 45.
21. Ibid.
22. Time. Oct. 30, 1978, p. 94.
23. Karol Wojytla, "Commentary on Decree on the Apostolate of the Laity," The Sixteen Documents of Vatican II. J.L. Gonzales, comp. (Boston: Daughter's of St. Paul, n.d.), p. 719.

24. Ed Grace, "Can John Paul Reform the Vatican?,"
    Christian Century. Jan. 31, 1979, p. 102.
25. Abbot, Documents of Vatican II. p. 77.
26. "Pope Renews Mandate Given to Cardinal Suenens,"
    New Covenant. April, 1979, p. 20.
27. Ibid.
28. Edward O'Connor, "The Hidden Roots of the
    Charismatic Renewal in the Catholic Church,"
    Aspects of Pentecostal-Charismatic Origins.
    Vinson Synan, ed. (Plainfield, N.J.: Logos
    International, 1975), p. 171.
29. Ibid.
30. Pope Leo XIII, "Divinium Illud," The Papal
    Encyclicals in Their Historical Context. Anne
    Fremantle, ed. (New York: Mentor-Omega Books,
    1956), p. 161.
31. O'Connor, "Hidden Roots," p. 173.
32. Ibid., p. 176.
33. Abbot, Documents of Vatican II. pp. 14-17.
34. Ibid., pp. 22-23.
35. De Ecclesia: The Constitution On The Church of
    Vatican Council II. Edward H. Peters, ed.
    (Glen Rock, N.J.: Deus Books, 1965), p. 23.
36. Ibid., p. 9.
37. Abbot, Documents of Vatican II. p. 23.
38. Peters, De Ecclesia. p. 10.
39. Léon Joseph Suenens, Essays on Renewal. (Ann
    Arbor, Mich.: Servant Books, 1977), pp. 95-96.
40. Abbot, Documents of Vatican II. pp. 25-27.
41. Ibid.
42. Ibid.
43. Ibid., p. 32.
44. Ibid., pp. 33-34.
45. Ibid., pp. 34-35.
46. Suenens, A New Pentecost?. p. xiii.
47. Oscar Cullman, Vatican Council II: The New
    Direction. (New York: Harper & Row, 1968),
    pp. 87-88.
48. Fichter, Catholic Cult. p. 3.
49. David Wells, Revolution in Rome. (Downers Grove,
    Ill.: InterVarsity Press, 1972), pp. 18-21.
50. Ibid., p. 20.
51. Yves Congar, The Meaning of Tradition. (New York:
    Hawthorn Books, 1964), p. 61.
52. Ibid.

53. Kilian McDonnell, The Charismatic Renewal and Ecumenism. (New York: Paulist Press, 1978), p. 73.
54. Fichter, Catholic Cult. p. 33.
55. George Martin, As the Spirit Leads Us. pp. 236-37.
56. Ibid., p. 245.
57. Francis A. Sullivan, "The Ecclesiological Context of the Charismatic Renewal," The Holy Spirit and Power: The Catholic Charismatic Renewal. Kilian McDonnell, ed. (New York: Doubleday, 1975), p. 129.
58. Congar, The Meaning of Tradition. p. 55.
59. Karl Rahner, interview with the author, Nov. 7, 1974.

CHAPTER V

CHARISMATIC RENEWAL AND ECUMENISM

Ecumenism properly understood is the noble
task of "agreeing while disagreeing" in the higher
interests of unity, community and testimony before
a watching world. The primary conciliar document
concerning ecumenism, Unitatis Reditegratio, represents a radical effort by the Church to reach
such a state. The decree focuses on the "pilgrim
Church" as a "people on the way," rather than espousing a mere "return" to the Catholic Church.[1]
The Church here went beyond exclusive and authoritative language to include in the body of Christ
all who are truly baptized and reborn:

> However, one cannot impute the sin of separa-
> tion to those who at present are born into
> these Communities and are instilled therein
> with Christ's faith. The Catholic Church
> accepts them with respect and affection as
> brothers. For men who believe in Christ and
> have been properly baptized are brought into
> a certain, though imperfect, communion with
> the Catholic Church. Undoubtedly, the differ-
> ences that exist in varying degrees between
> them and the Catholic Church--whether in doc-
> trine and sometimes in discipline, or con-
> cerning the structure of the Church--do indeed
> create many and sometimes serious obstacles
> to full ecclesiastical communion. These the
> ecumenical community is striving to overcome.
> Nevertheless, all those justified by faith
> through baptism are incorporated into Christ.
> They therefore have a right to be honored by
> the title of Christian, and are properly re-
> garded as brothers in the Lord by the sons of
> the Catholic Church.[2]

This statement of agreement was then
followed by a statement of disagreement:

Nevertheless, our separated brethren,
whether considered as individuals or as Communities

and Churches, are not blessed with that unity
which Jesus Christ wished to bestow on all
those whom He has regenerated and vivified
into one body and newness of life--that unity
which the Holy Scriptures and the revered tradition of the Church proclaim. For it is
through Christ's Catholic Church alone, which
is the all-embracing means of salvation, that
the fullness of the means of salvation can be
obtained. It was to the apostolic college
alone, of which Peter is the head, that we believe our Lord entrusted all the blessings of
the New Covenant, in order to establish on
earth the one Body of Christ into which all
those should be fully incorporated who already
belong in any way to God's People.[3]

Such a frank statement of polarity would
seem to provide a healthy atmosphere for ecumenical dialogue--goals and differences are plainly
stated. To be sure, dialogue did take place,
ecumenism did work--but it operated in reverse.
Andrew Greeley states that approximately 6,000
priests and 25,000 nuns have left their religious
vocations in the past decade.[4] David J. O'Brien
notes:

In a real sense, the ecumenical movement
has reached a dead end. Most young Christians
have little concern with ecumenism considered
as inter-Christian dialogue and movements toward church unity. While they may follow
developments in this field with varying degrees
of interest, their most pressing concerns lie
elsewhere. For one thing their emotional in-
vestment in denominational institutions is
slight. Participation in parish or specifically
denominational organizations is minimal. Lacking, for better or worse, deep personal commitment to formal church structures, they tend to
minimize doctrinal differences among Christians,
a tendency reinforced for Catholics by a break-
down of old certitudes and the resurgence of an
equally venerable stress on love and community,

vague terms less susceptible to self-righteous
partisanship than the virgin birth or papal
infallibility.[5]

According to Will Herberg:

The church was not in any special crisis when
the Second Vatican Council was convened in
1962. On the contrary, it was in a particularly flourishing state, institutionally, intellectually, and religiously. As John Lukacs
pointed out in 1959 (in his introduction to
Alexis de Tocqueville's The European Revolution),
"for the first time since the Counter-Reformation, conversions have been flowing almost
unilaterally toward Catholicism." But today,
after the Council, the entire trend has been
reversed: institutionally, intellectually,
religiously, the Church is under attack, is
falling back, is in crisis.[6]

These statements, to be sure, reflect a
spiritual and social analysis of Catholicism as
well as ecumenical concern. But both elements,
ecumenism and religious revival or lapse, are
wedded to one another. The hierarchical structure
of Catholicism contains a basic polarity between
authority and faith, clergy and laity. All churches
have the same polar ingredients in terms of leadership and service, but Catholicism has a greater tension due to its emphasis on apostolicity and infallibility.

In order for revival or ecumenism to succeed
in Catholicism, both elements, the led as well as
the leaders, must be in harmony. For the leaders,
significant gains have been made. Vatican II,
subsequent dialogue with Eastern and Anglican
Churches, and improvement in Jewish relations are
important matters not to be deemphasized in the
quest for unity. The problem, however, is that
the sheep have not followed. Ecumenism necessitates
a committed and consistent laity. To engage in
dialogue with a half-hearted constituency is the

71

height of folly. The very nature of ecumenism pre-
supposes disagreement as well as agreement. Commitment to opposites is necessary. For both evangelism
and ecumenism to bear fruit one must be able to point
out credible Christian communities. One must be able
to say, "This is living Christianity. Come and see
for yourselves. If you would experience these communities you would believe."[7]

        Kilian McDonnell asks: "Where does one find
those fraternities and sororities of Christians
which have been seized by the gospel, whose members
are committed to the Lord and to each other in such
a way as to cause others to wonder? The community
of committed Christians is the primary locus of
evangelization."[8] The problem is that the renewal
promised by Vatican II never took place. "At the
level where most persons experience the church,
that is the local community, it is the want of holiness, the lack of fruit, and the manifest disunity
which make her efforts at evangelization ineffective
and constitutes a threat to the power of the gospel."[9]

        The most basic explanation for this lack
of revival is that the period following Vatican II
gave way to a religious externalism devoid of true
spiritual revival:

        To point to a specific area in the post-
        conciliar period where change was conceived
        too externally, there was a working assumption,
        never articulated, that if one found the right
        form of liturgical celebration, the right evoc-
        ative language, the appropriate architectural
        setting, and finally, if one could find a priest
        who had a sense of celebration, then everything
        would fall into place and it would happen:
        people would commit their lives to Christ and
        be transformed by the Holy Spirit. That never
        happened. At least it never happened in a
        broad, patterned way. This liturgical exter-
        nalism was never promoted by professional litur-
        gists but was found at the parish level.[10]

The Charismatic Renewal sees itself as a corrective to this lack through its emphasis on individual spiritual reality:

We must recognize that it is not in books or in archives that separated Christians hope to find this spiritual renewal, this candor, this doctrinal and dynamic poise. Nor is it even in the schemas of Vatican II. They hope to find them, before all else, in the commnity of the faithful, as it exists and as it thinks and prays and acts. It is through the body of Catholics as a whole and through each individual Catholic, through their spirituality, their ideas, their attitudes, that Protestants and Orthodox come into contact with Catholicism. It is the entire body of Catholics and each individual Catholic who trace out, by all that they are and all that they do, the characteristic features of the Church as seen by the separated brethren. To put it briefly, just as we judge Lutheranism on the basis of the image Lutherans present, and not merely on the basis of professions of faith, so too do Protestants judge Catholicism in the light of the image presented by the members of the Catholic community. During a period of ecumenism, every Catholic must assume an awesome responsibility, for he stands for the whole Church.[11]

In addition to its individual spiritual contribution the renewal also sees itself as providing perhaps the only consistent meeting ground for Christians of varying faiths. This meeting place is "the surprising convergence of the Christian Churches toward the Holy Spirit, who is, as it were, our meeting point, at the same time, on the levels of spirituality, doctrine and development."[12] Pope Paul VI stated unequivocally that the work of Vatican II was to be succeeded by a more developed pneumatology which would serve as "an indispensable complement of the teaching of the council."[13] Suenens maintains that, "Any development in pneumatology on the doctrinal level, is of its very nature, moving in the direction of ecumenical union. This does not mean, however, that we can meet on common ground--and this is important."14 The Holy Spirit is thus viewed as a doctrinal meeting place where crucial issues can be discussed.15 According to Kevin Ranaghan:

> We now see Catholics, evangelicals, and fundamentalists sitting down together around the Word in a common experience of salvation to praise our Father with one voice in unity and love. Our unity is by no means complete. We still have many differences in doctrine and practice. But the unity we share in faith in Jesus, in praise of the Father, and in the life of the Holy Spirit is genuine. Thus, what we have been unable to accomplish by ourselves has been worked among us by the Holy Spirit.

Stephen Clark maintains that:

> If we want to follow what the Lord is doing in the church today and in the charismatic renewal today, we in the Catholic charismatic renewal, have to have an ecumenical concern. The unity with other Christians that we experience is something the Lord wants to have continue. He is moving all Christians towards a oneness of brotherly communion and service, and we should be open to following his leading.17

Ecumenical concern means two things to renewalists: (1) concern for spiritual renewal in churches other than Catholic and, (2) an integral and open support for the ecumenical unity of all Christians.18 The latter concern prevents overemphasis on spiritual ecumenism which might neglect social, economic and political factors. Still, the main contribution of the Renewal has to be the spiritual base or motivation for the external union:

> To dwell on spiritual ecumenism does not mean to overlook the importance of ecumenical action in other sectors, such as the social,

74

the economic or the political. But Providence seems to be assigning to the Charismatic Renewal a specific role, full of promise for the future, by making it the instrument of brotherly and profound encounters between Christians, united in a "preservering and unanimous" prayer--a prayer whose prototype was that of the Cenacle in Jerusalem on the eve of Pentecost.[19]

Having established the spiritual contribution of charismatic renewal to the ecumenical arena, the question remains whether the renewal is truly congruent with the definitions and interests of ecumenism. It must always be remembered that ecumenism is dialectical in nature--its Christian witness comes not only from agreement, but from disagreement. This means that there is a vast difference between ecumenism and "non-denominationalism." Non-denominational meetings are based solely on areas of agreement--Christians unite on the basis of a common "core" of beliefs. Ecumenical gatherings occur, conversely, when persons cross sectarian lines on the basis not only of common faith but also the lack of complete unity in faith.[20] When prayer groups or inter-denominational gatherings take place on the basis of commonality in worship, to share a "common faith", this does not mean that ecumenism is taking place:

In a real sense (these groups) do not come together specifically to further the purposes of the ecumenical movement, though these gatherings do advance the movement toward the unity of the churches. But that advance is a by-product, a very real and desirable one, but a by-product, nonetheless. One does not have in these gatherings a dialogue situation, clearly ecumenical, which exists when two or more churches come together in an offical way with professionally competent theologians to study areas of agreement and disagreement. In this kind of dialogue ecumenism, the unity of the churches, is not a by-product but the main purpose of the gathering.[21]

75

McDonnell urges that national, regional
and local meetings should be ecumenical in character, implying that the absence of disagreement
does not represent the true interests of ecumenism,
". . . the dominant character of the overall way
in which Protestants, Anglicans, Orthodox and Roman
Catholic relate to one another should be ecumenical
rather than non-denominational."[22] The implication
is that absence of honest disagreement is not representative of the true interests of ecumenism.
Further, that as a general norm national, regional
and local meetings should be specifically ecumenical in character.[23] Some expression of division
is necessary to avoid a vague "churchless" Christianity.[24]

The question is whether the Charismatic
Renewal has maintained a truly ecumenical profile.
In both action and thought renewalists project more
of a non-denominational identity than a Catholic
identity. Josephine Ford states:

In biblical times "tongues" were a sign
of international unity and a sign of the extension of the Christian message to all peoples.
Today it may be the same profound and dynamic
prophetic symbol--a prophetic oth of interde-
nominational unity [italics mine] . It may
be a sign to Christian denominations that they
have much to give to and receive from each
other, but also much in common. It is not without significance that the charismatic renewal
began shortly after Pope Leo XIII's Encyclical
on the Holy Spirit, the non-Roman Catholic
prayers for unity, and then Vatican Council II,
which was preceded by the earnest prayer of
the Church for a New Pentecost.[25]

Edward O'Connor also describes the unity
of the Spirit as non-denominational in nature:

When the charismatic renewal, after having
been confined for decades to the Pentecostal
denominations, began to penetrate into the
established churches, it naturally tended to
create bonds among all those who embraced it.
These were not, however, bonds of doctrinal

agreement; for it is not the spread of <u>ideas</u> about the Holy Spirit that constitute the Pentecostal movement, but <u>experience</u> of the Spirit's powerful action. The bonds established have been those of personal love.[26]

The position of the Holy Spirit in such a framework is to serve as the lowest common denominator for a Christian fellowship. But unity on the basis of such subjective experience seems contradictory to the highest nature of ecumenism.

Cardinal Johannes Willebrands clearly defined this non-denominational character of charismatic renewal in his 1975 address to the International Congress on the Catholic Charismatic Renewal held in Rome:

You ask me, as President of the Secretariat for Unity, where the ecumenical importance of the Charismatic Renewal lies? In my view, its ecumenical significance is beyond doubt. The Charismatic Renewal was born and has grown in the very midst of the People of God. . . it regards itself as a movement of the Spirit, a call to <u>spiritual</u> <u>ecumenism</u> [italics mine] . In every sector we need ecumenical activities-- contacts, dialogues, colloboration--stemming from the spiritual source which is conversion, holiness of life, public and private prayer, in order to achieve Christian Unity.[27]

Cardinal Suenens describes the 1977 Charismatic Convention in Kansas City as "the most impressive ecumenical manifestation of our time"[28]

At this Congress some 50,000 Christians-- of whom nearly half were Catholics--met together; each group held a denominational meeting in the morning, but in the evening all the groups gathered in the stadium and movingly expressed their deep longing for unity. There Catholics, Baptists, Episcopalians, Lutherans, Mennonites, Pentecostals, Presbyterians, United Methodists, Messianic Jews and a non-denominational Protestant group, greeted one another with warmth and joy and prayed together. Bearing in mind the history of the strained relations between the Christian confessions in the United States, this Congress was epoch-making, the realization of "an impossible dream."[29]

Viewed from the standpoint of a highly developed ecumenism, then, the Renewal seems to lack the healthy tension of disagreement. Because of its subjectivity it may even be counter-productive. Kilian McDonnell warns that there is a "flow of Catholics" to Protestant charismatic churches:

> Certain tensions arise when persons from one ecclesiastical tradition pass over into another. There are, for instance, charismatic prayer groups or churches which are dominantly Protestant and are identifiable as belonging to either historic Protestantism, to classical Pentecostalism, or to an independent non-denominational free ministry. Catholics who come into contact with these groups often experience a vibrant, vital Christian life, which has the power to transform lives. Usually it is the total communication experience, and not any attempt at proselytism, which is so convincing. Sometimes people get fed spiritually here in a way they never experienced before in their own Catholic parish. In a rather immediate, personal way they are exposed to an evangelization which confronts them with the living God, and the power of the gospel.[30]

While no statistics are available, a sufficient number of Catholics have left, usually through ecumenical prayer groups, to warrant a warning against being proselytized.[31] Conversely, McDonnell notes some drift from Protestantism to Catholicism via the dominantly Catholic prayer groups or communities.[32] It would seem that the Spirit authenticates the majority party in the group, be it

78

Catholic or Protestant. It seems logical to con-
clude that the extreme charismatic emphasis on experience precludes true ecumenical dialogue in
favor of subjective fellowship.

There is another area, however, in which
the charismatic renewal could make a genuine contribution to ecumenism. The heart of the ecumenical
problem lies not in the decree on ecumenism, Unitatis Reditegratio, but rather in the Council's
definition of the Church in Lumen Gentium. One
might say that the former is a statement of possibilities while the latter contains the central
obstacle. Perhaps the clearest statement of the
problem was made by Edmund Schlink of Heidelberg
in comments concerning Vatican II on October 23,
1963:

> Professor Schlink started with the premise
> that the "Roman Church" . . .identified itself
> in an exclusive manner with the one, holy,
> catholic and apostolic Church. Whenever Rome
> recognized a bond between individual non-
> Catholic Christians and the Church this im-
> plied that these Christians considered them-
> selves united with the Roman Church. Schlink,
> however, insisted that these Christians saw
> themselves as receiving grace and salvation as
> members of their own Churches and not as mem-
> bers of the Roman Church. Not only did the
> Catholic position misinterpret the self-aware-
> ness of non-Catholic Christians; it was also
> out of line with the New Testament. Finally,
> it followed with unavoidable logic from this
> position that non-Roman Christians were re-
> quired to "leave their Churches and be incor-
> porated into the Roman Church." These obser-
> vations led Professor Schlink to ask: "What
> is the meaning then of Roman Catholic ecumen-
> ism? What is the meaning of the new way of
> addressing non-Roman Christians as 'separated
> brethren' instead of as 'heretics' and
> 'schismatics' as in the past? What is the
> meaning of the praise given to the 'spiritual
> fruits' to be found in non-Roman Churches, and

79

what is meant by 'accepting the witness of
their devotion. . .and their theological
insights'? Is not all this an effort aimed
at absorption? Is not this kind of ecumenism,
as some Protestant Christians suspect, merely
a continuation of the Counter-Reformation with
other, more accommodating methods?"[33]

The solution posed by Schilink was a different
concept of ecumenism. He urged that the movement
become a matter of community rather than absorption.[34] Each individual church would be a con-
cretization of the universal church which has no
actual existence.

Although Vatican II is truly epochal in
its recognition of the legitimacy of other Christian Churches, the essence of Romanism is that the
Church really exists. The visible Church is the
actual dwelling place of God among men. The only
plurality of Churches is a multiplicity of Churches
within the framework of the one and visible Church,
geographically or chronologically separated congregations unified by Table and Bishop.[35] Joseph
Ratzinger cautions that New Testament plurality of
Churches does not mean separated denominational
communities, but rather many worshipping communities
"which are all nonetheless one."[36]

The ecumenical movement grew out of a situation
unknown to the New Testament and for which the
New Testament can therefore offer no guidelines.
The plurality of Churches, which should have
had a legitimate existence within the Church,
had receded increasingly into the background.
This explains why this plurality, for which
there was no room within the Church, was developed outside of it in the form of autonomous
separate Churches. The Council's recognition
of this is tantamount to its seeing that uniformity and unity are not identical. Above
all, it means that a real multiplicity of
Churches must be made alive again within the
framework of Catholic unity.[37]

Ratzinger is searching for a synthesis which will both release the tension between unity and uniformity and answer Schlink. Here the charismatic renewal could make a distinctive contribution. Vatican II contains the seeds for a looser view of Church structure which, if followed, could give Rome a new ecumenical identity. The nature of this trend of thought is amply illustrated by the theological innovation of Hans Küng. Speaking of the "pluriform Church," he first maintains that it is the Catholics, not the Protestants, who have misunderstood the nature of the Church by emphasizing its unity in a manner which makes individual congregations an inferior part of a superior whole.[38] Catholics today, he states, recognize that the local Church is not just a "section" or "province" of the universal Church, but rather that the Church is wholly present in every place that the local Church exists:

> No, the local Church does not merely belong to the Church. The local Church is the Church and can fully represent the cause of Jesus Christ. It is only in the light of the local Church and its concrete realization that the light of the local Church and its concrete realization that the universal Church can be understood. But it is really the Church to which is promised and given in its own place everything it needs there for men's salvation: the proclamation of the Gospel, baptism, the eucharist, the different charisms and ministries.[39]

Protestants, in the second place, are recogninzing that their externally diverse groups have a common spiritual essence which constitutes their diversity as "a Church of Jesus Christ."[40] One might say that both sides are advancing toward their opposites and will meet in the middle. The conclusion of these two "drifts" (could one describe Protestantism as searching for unity and Catholicism as searching for essence?) is a concept of the Church which could revolutionize ecumenism:

81

Through all this--and what could be more
important for them?--they are not merely externally linked, but inwardly united. They
all form not only an ecclesiastical organization, but a Church of Jesus Christ. The
Church is not an umbrella association of individual congregations. The ecclesia is not
the sum total of the individual ecclesiae;
the ecclesia cannot be broken down into the
individual ecclesiae. But it is the ecclesia
of God in different places.[41]

These two recognitions, when merged, would
result in the following synthesis:

Each ecclesia, each assembly, congregation,
Church--however small, insignificant, mediocre,
wretched--fully represents the ecclesia, the
assembly, congregation, Church of God and of
Jesus Christ. All this holds both for a
lonely mission station in the African bush
and for a large prosperous parish in the
American Middle West or in Central Europe,
both for a parish on a new housing estate and
for a regional parish uniting several former
village parishes. This is true . . . finally
for congregations in the Catholic or Orthodox
or in one or another Protestant tradition
(with increasing integration and--we may
hope--eventual mutual recognition). In all
their diversity and multiplicity all these
can truly be called "Church."[42]

It is the latter part of this statement
that is notable. Küng actually advances a view of
the Church which contradicts the exclusiveness of
Romanism. Elsewhere he writes:

The unity of the Church has nothing to do
with the mythological magic of the number one
and the intrinsic fascination of oneness. The
unity of the Church is not simply a natural
entity, is not simply moral unanimity and
harmony, is not just sociological conformity
and uniformity. To judge it by externals
(canon law, ecclesiastical language, Church

administration, etc.) is to misunderstand it
completely. The unity of the Church is a
spiritual entity. It is not chiefly a unity
of the members among themselves, it depends
finally not on itself but on the unity of
God, which is efficacious through Jesus Christ
in the Holy Spirit.[43]

Küng may be considered a radical theologian but his terms and definitions are fully
supported by Vatican II. In current Catholic
thinking the Church as a spiritual reality, and
hence unity as a spiritual ecumenism, has gained
ascendence over the Church as an historical
reality, and hence ecumenicity as absorption.
McDonnell observes:

The Council moved away from a simple and
exclusive identification between the church
of Jesus Christ and the Roman Catholic church.
The phrase "churches and ecclesial communities"
is used of Protestant groups, but the theological commission of set purpose did not indicate
to whom "church" applied and its usage neither
affirmed nor denied that they were churches
in the theological sense.[44]

Because of such ambiguity, an increasing
number of Catholic theologians have been speaking
on "other" Churches in terms which would put them
on a par with Rome.[45] Yves Congar urges Christians to "a conception of the Church as "fellowship" and, "at an even deeper level, to a dis-
covery of pneumatology:"

A Christianity of fellowship, a more
dynamic conception of unity as something to
be constantly recreated, as awareness of the
forms already established when compared with
the purity and depth and fullness to which we
are called (for the Holy Spirit ceaselessly
urges us on and calls us to progress well beyond our present achievements!), would enable
us to embrace a pluralism and even the pressing requests--often so rich in their promise

83

of progress--of so many Christians who, at present, are no longer finding enough oxygen in the established structures.[46]

While the comments of Catholic theologians do not carry the weight of papal authority, their feelings are supported by the language and tone of Vatican II documents. The change in perspective concerning the Church, negative in its lack of internal coherency or consistency, becomes positive in its ecumenical and evangelical application. The charismatic renewal is capable of effectively utilizing this "drift" in a way that no other contemporary renewal has or could to effect a new direction in ecumenism. Léon Suenens states that," . . . in hindsight we perceive that the deep waters of the ecumenical current and the charismatic current lend strength to one another, and that we are dealing with one and the same action, one and the same impulse of God, one and the same internal logic."[47]

The charismatic thesis is that spiritual renewal is a "prerequisite of ecumenism and hence precedes it."[48] Ecumenism properly conceived is held to be the movement of Christians toward unity through both mission and spiritual renewal. The charismatic renewal thus sees itself as a second "stream," not necessarily precedent chronologically but at least concomitant with the stream of ecumenism. The rationale would be as follows. First, the renewal would define its theological base as trinitarian.[49] The Church is identified as an ecclesial "we" only because the same Holy Spirit is in Christ and the Church.[50] "Because the same Spirit dwells in both Christ and the Church," the Christian community can be called "Christ."[51]

The Church is the result of two missions, that of Christ and that of the Spirit. Christ and the Spirit constitute the Church in the same moment, and there is no temporal priority of either Christ or the Spirit. This in no way compromises the truth that the initial life of the Church in Jesus' ministry receives a new modality and force at Pentecost.[52]

The Church, therefore, is not simple an extension of the Incarnation.[53]

The theological point is that just as God's true unity can only be accurately perceived as a fellowship of persons, so also the unity of the Church can only be perceived accurately as a fellowship. "The Spirit gathers into unity because it is the Spirit who constitutes the Church as the body of Christ."[54] The Vatican II definition of the Church as "a people on the way", the community of the faithful, is therefore exactly in keeping with charismatic renewal emphasis on community and identification of the Church by such elements. According to Suenens,

It is natural that we should look to this primordial unity which commands our unity in the Church: the trinitarian unity. The ecclesial unity that we must try to restore as a visible reality should reflect the plural unity of God himself. At one time our theology so stressed the oneness of God that we ran the risk of looking upon him as unipersonal, and this had serious repercussions in our understanding of the Church as "the image of God."[55]

Heribert Mühlen states, "The Charismatic Renewal is God's response to what was called for in Vatican II as regards a more collegial, brotherly, communal way of making decisions and exercising authority in the church. . ."[56] As a result of this fellowship:

Countless Christians now living the experience of the Charismatic Renewal see it as a fulfillment, among others, of that bold ecumenical hope of the Council. There is much evidence that the Renewal belong to those

inspirations of the Spirit which the Council
intuitively foresaw for the future. The history of the Church is made up of those movements and embraces of the Spirit, which are
given periodically to revitalize the Church.
The Renewal is to be seen as an extension of
that current of graces which was and remains
Vatican II.[57]

The second ingredient of the renewal's
contribution to ecumenism would deal with the
major question of doctrinal disagreement, the tension between the Church of the Spirit and the
Church of history, between unity and uniformity.
It must be said at the outset that this problem
of pluralism has never really been answered. Regardless of talk about community and "spiritual
ecumenism" Catholics must identify with the
Church which is continuous with the history of
the Catholic Church. Separated Churches are not
equally legitimate manifestations of the Church.[58]
"The Catholic Church believes that in a concrete
historical way she is the Church of Jesus Christ,
the covenant people, the body of Christ. The
Church of Jesus subsists in her, which means to
be present in a concrete historical way."[59]

The problem here is that Vatican II has
not spoken in a way which grants equality to
separated Churches, thus preserving the ecumenical
tension over absorption:

The Council moved away from a simple and
exclusive identification between the church
of Jesus Christ and the Roman Catholic church.
The phrase "churches and ecclesial communities"
is used of Protestant groups, but the theological commission of set purpose did not indicate
to whom "church" applied and its usage neither
affirmed nor denied that they were churches in
the theological sense. . . In a summary way one
can say that Vatican II moved away from the
simple and exclusive identification of the
church of Jesus Christ with the Catholic church;

it recognized that something of the substance
of the church exists outside of her visible
boundaries, but did not arrive at the point of
applying the term "church" in the theological
sense to Protestant denominations. Clearly,
this is an ambiguous situation which perhaps
reflects the unresolved state of the theological questions at the time of the Council.[60]

So although an ever increasing number of Catholic
thinkers fully recognize Protestants, the "official
Roman church has not taken over such usage."[61]

The charismatic renewal feels it can bridge
this gap by emphasizing the Church as a mystery:

It is noteworthy that the Vatican Council
did not begin its treatment of the Church with
the people of God, as is frequently but errone-
ously asserted. The Council began with the
Church as mystery. It was the Church as mystery
which was to underlie the whole conciliar
teaching. It is a reality hidden in God, made
manifest in Christ Jesus and spread abroad in
the power of the Holy Spirit.[62]

Within this context the unity of the Church is to
be understood in a "dynamic" sense, as a "force
emanting from the Holy Spirit infused in the
Church."[63] Consequently,

The unity of the Church, then, is compatible with a pluralism on the liturgical,
canonical and spiritual planes. But it uncom-
promising requires a fundamental unity in faith.
I do not say in theology, for provided that
the faith is safe and intact, the Church wel-
comes a plurality of theologies. It is therefore important to emphasize a common faith as
an essential requirement of unity.[64]

Terms have still not been clarified. For
example, are Orthodox and separated brethren being
welcomed? What does "welcome" mean? The flow of
thought is definitely toward an experientially

based encounter at the expense of theology and
history. Suenens, one of the authors of the
"people of God" theme for Vatican II,[65] regards
the first condition for ecumenism as supernatural
authenticity.[66] "Supernatural ecumenism" would be
that which springs from prayer and mutual confession
of past hurts.[67] But the question remains whether
the supernatural is being utilized as a category
with which one may bypass doctrine and history.
Suenens reminds us that, "The Church of Christ is
one. But its unity dwells in the depths of
mystery."[68] The Church is described as having an
existence, or "consistence," "which precedes and
transcends the conscious adherence of believers
to Jesus Christ and to the particular community
of which they are members.[69] The "mystical
unity" of the Church cannot be impaired by men;
it is the "universal sacrament of salvation."[70]
Suenens regards the latter term of "sacrament" as
having the richest implications of all definitions
for the Church.[71]

As long as the Christian does not welcome,
in faith, the very mystery of the Church, he
remains on the level of history and not of the
dogma and Creed which proclaim "the one, holy,
catholic and apostolic Church." This Church
is indeed the original one: that of the
Cenacle of the first Pentecost.[72]

It is necessary, therefore, that Christians re-read Acts together in order to seep themselves in the faith of the first Christians, "for
whom the Holy Spirit was a primordial and personal
reality."[73] In the words of Edouard Schweitzer,
"Long before the Holy Spirit became an article of
the Creed, he was a reality lived in the experience
of the primitive Church."[74] Consequently, "In
concrete terms, this ecclesiology is today a lived
experience, in the charismatic renewal and elsewhere. . ."[75]

Clearly, this keener awareness of the
Holy Spirit, which is visibly awakening today
in the Church, is essential to a true ecumeni-

cal spirit, which rests on a radical openness
to the Spirit of God and to our partners in
the dialogue. As Pope Paul VI declared in
his address of April 28, 1967, to the members
of the Secretariat for Christian unity: "If
there is one cause in which our human efficacy
proves powerless to achieve a good result and
shows itself to be essentially dependent on the
mysterious and powerful action of the Holy
Spirit, it is surely that of ecumenism.[76]

This type of "spiritual ecumenism,"
emphasizing the mysterious, sacramental and spiritual
nature of the ecclesia, simply bypasses the questions of doctrine and history! Subjectivity once
again becomes truth and division seems to disappear.
The question is whether the charismatic solution
is a valid option for the Catholic Church. For one
thing, movements which attempt to "rediscover" the
Acts experience present the same problems as Tri-
dentine Catholicism. If Acts is anything it is
historical! The experience of Acts is meaningful
only as event--and this involves the question of
the organization, nature and identity of the early
ecclesia. To follow the path of pentecostal experience in Acts is to encounter history with a
vengence. The problems of pluralism are ignored
rather than solved.

This is not to say, however, that the
Catholic Church will be bound by historical or
philosophical laws of consistency. If anything,
the Catholic Church is a Church which changes--
its view of revelation permits the possibility of
continued development. Accordingly, the charismatic renewal may serve as a catalyst for any number of changes. For example, the Church's testimony of unity has often been hindered by tension
between progressive and conservative parties within the Church. If these parties choose to unite
around subjective experience, any synthesis becomes
possible. The charismatic renewal demonstrates
this principle in that,". . .by entirely different
routes and for entirely different reason, charis-

matic and liberal Catholic have arrived at much
the same point. For both, inner realities are
taking precedence over outward authority."[77]

The problem with subjectivity as a "point
of contact" is the same for Catholic charismatics
as for the entire charismatic renewal movement,
namely, when renewal has finally taken place, when
differences have finally been "forgotten" and revival has taken place, just what kind of Church
does one have? We are forced to return not to
ecumenism, but to non-denominationalism, to
McDonnell's "Churchless Christianity." Within such
a context one can have a religious experience, but
it becomes impossible to interpret such experience!

On the other hand, the charismatic renewal could provide a positive and necessary contribution to Rome--provided the Church is prepared
to adopt a new terminology and definition of its
nature. The seed for such a possible new direction
is the increasing recognition of a "pluriform" or
"multiform" dimension of the Church. Although
Vatican II was ambiguous concerning the exact
standing of "separated Churches", Rome is very
close to granting equality in principle if not in
fact.

Added to this is the fact that the radical
nature of Vatican II in departing from previous
categories has lent an unseen impetus to the more
radical theologians. It is reasonable to suppose
that innovation of radicalism (depending on one's
perspective) will proliferate as the Church drifts
without her classical anchors.

When these factors are focused on such historical problems as infallibility and ecclesiastical authority, new religious reasoning can take
place. Küng, for example, would see the historical
tensions over Petrine primacy as the product of
social and political forces which distorted the true
nature of the question. At the First Vatican
Council the Church defined papal primacy and infallibility in reaction to "anti-Gallican and anti-liberal

attitudes."[78] Vatican II displayed an entirely different attitude because it was clear that "new definitions of ancient truths were of no use to the Church's proclamation of the faith in the modern world."[79]

The answer, Küng writes, is to view papal primacy outside of the context of history, as a matter dealing more with the Church's essence than the Church's existence:

But the important thing about a Petrine ministry or any other ministry of leadership is not the historical evidence of a live of succession. What really matters is succession in spirit: that is, in the Petrine mission and task, in the Petrine testimony and service.[80]

The meaning of this emphasis is to de-emphasize concrete historical difficulties by emphasizing the spiritual nature and task of Church office. The question of whether one has an authentic "geneology" becomes completely secondary to the "spiritual" question of whether an individual has "lived up to the Petrine mission as described in Scriptures."[81] Kung hypothesizes that even if such a person could not verify an historical claim--that if it were indeed impossible to link his ministry with a specific source, that even if it were impossible to check on commissions or appointments made 2,000 years ago, still,

If this other person lived up to the Petrine mission as described in Scripture, if he fulfilled mandate and task and performed this service to the Church, would it not then be a secondary--although still important--question whether the "genealogy" of this authentic servant of the Church was in order? Perhaps he would then not have an irreproachable line of succession, but he would have the charism of leadership (kyberneseis) and this would basically suffice.[82]

91

Thus the important thing is not one's "right" or claim to succession, but rather, "the accomplishment, the exercise, the action, the service itself completely realized."[83]

The methodology here seems to be that of simply living in a halfway house between subjectivity and objectivity, holding one's historicity in one hand and one's spiritual essence in the other. The result of such an approach is not so much that history is denied, but that it is simply made irrelevant. One is reminded of Bultmann's approach to the resurrection--the validity of the event is not historical, but spiritual. The resurrection is proved by the Easter faith rather than the empty tomb; indeed, the latter is superflous. The same approach is here offered the Church--a spiritual reality and validity as opposed to a historical reality and validity.

Of course one may question whether the Church would opt for such a solution. It is very difficult to "climb out of history", and perhaps threatening to do so. But why could the Church not decide on just such a course? The documents of Vatican II are replete with references supporting seeming contradictions. The very view of revelation advanced by Catholicism makes such a process possible. It would seem that any religion possessing a dualistic concept of revelation would of necessity find itself living somewhere between the two polarities.

As to whether the risk should be taken, Küng urges that the Church see its present situation as a "way back" from the "primacy of domination to the ancient primacy of service."[84] To change direction or emphasis toward the "power of servitude" would require a courageous ganble, namely, that the Church accept a "voluntary renunciation of spiritual power."[85] Küng states that what seem politically unreasonable, "even in terms of Church politics", may be required if the Church is to follow the example of Jesus:

Without the renunciation of "spiritual" power neither a reunion of the separated Christian Churches nor a radical renewal of the Catholic

Church in the light of the Gospel is possible.
There is nothing natural about the renunciation
of power. Why should a person, an authority,
an institution, give up something it already
possesses without being assured of anything in
return? Renunciation of power is in fact possible
only for someone who has grasped something of
the message of Jesus and the Sermon on the Mount.[86]

Some would feel it unlikely that Rome would
take such a risk--but is it really? What would
Rome have to lose by making such a "renunciation"?
If the Church chooses to live in categories of
synthesis rather than antithesis, why can it not do
so? Within the context of charismatic renewal it
is a simple matter to overlook antithesis on the
basis of experience, to provide just such a "renunciation" of power without damaging one's counter-
claim to historicity. Charismatic religious experience is a dialectical button which when pushed is
capable of fusing even the most polar elements.

The charismatic renewal contains the synthe-
sizing element sought by progressive theologians.
Given the current religious atmosphere in Catholicism
created by failure of previous Vatican II reforms,
the contribution of the charismatic renewal, the
installation of a new, dynamic and different Pope,
the unceasing pressure from progressives and the
acceptance of relativity via Vatican II, one may
project that the Catholic Church will make dramatic
changes to effect ecumenism in this decade. The
Pope will accept new and compromising definitions
concerning papal infallibility, as will the church
concerning apostolicity. "Spiritual" ecumenism and
ecclesial "essence" will become words of challenge
to Protestants who have historically resisted over-
tures on the basis of doctrinal and historical
questions.

Again, what does Rome really have to lose
by such an attempt? Secularism has been a constant
enemy, as have those Churches or movements displaying
a spiritual life seemingly superior to Catholicism.

Even more important, Vatican II has cut Rome adrift by holding out for an implicit decentralization. One might say it has placed the Church in "process" that demands a conclusion. At present the Church needs a compass by which it may chart its direction. The destination, of course, is Vatican III and the Church of tomorrow. What that Church is to be, and is now becoming, will be due in no small part to the spiritual option provided by the charismatic renewal.

NOTES

1. Documents of Vatican II. p. 338.
2. Ibid., p. 345.
3. Ibid., p. 346
4. Ann Landers, "How Many Priests, Nuns Have Quit? "Houston Chronicle", March 16, 1979, p. 8. A full compilation of statistics may be found in Greeley's The American Catholic: A Social Portrait. (New York: Basic Books, 1977), pp. 126-163.
5. David J. O'Brien, The Renewal of American Catholicism. (New York: Paulist Press by special arrangement with Oxford University Press, 1972), p. 133.
6. Garry Wills, Bare Ruined Choirs: Doubt, Prophecy, and Radical Religion. (New York: Dell Pub., A Delta Book, 1971), p. 253.
7. Kilian McDonnell, Charismatic Renewal and Ecumenism. (New York: Paulist Press, 1978), p. 17.
8. Ibid., p. 18
9. Ibid., p. 17
10. Ibid., p. 12
11. Leon Suenens, Essays on Renewal. (Ann Arbor: Servant Books, 1977), pp. 107-108.
12. Suenens, A New Pentecost?, p. 184.
13. Ibid., p. 188.
14. Ibid.
15. Ibid., p. 189.
16. As the Spirit Leads Us, p. 116.
17. Stephen Clark, Where Are We Headed?, p. 25.
18. Ibid., p. 25.
19. Leon Joseph Suenens, Ecumenism and Charismatic Renewal: Theological and Pastoral Orientations. (Ann Arbor: Servant Books, 1978).
20. McDonnell, Charismatic Renewal and Ecumenism, p. 79.
21. Ibid.
22. Ibid.
23. Ibid.
24. Ibid.
25. Josephine Ford, "Toward a Theology of 'Speaking in Tongues,'" Theological Studies 32, (March 1971), p. 29.
26. Edward D. O'Connor, Pentecost in the Modern World. (Notre Dame, Indiana: Ave Maria Press, 1972), p. 33.
27. Suenens, Ecumenism and Charismatic Renewal: Theological and Pastoral Orientations. pp. 22-23.
28. Ibid.
29. Ibid.

30. McDonnell, Charismatic Renewal and Ecumenism. p. 67.
31. Ibid., pp. 67-69.
32. Ibid., pp. 69.
33. Ratzinger, Theological Highlights of Vatican II,
    pp. 69-70.
34. Ibid., p. 70.
35. Ibid., p. 71.
36. Ibid., pp. 71-72.
37. Ibid., p. 72.
38. Hans Küng, On Being a Christian, Translated by
    Edward Quinn (New York: Doubleday, 1976), p. 480.
39. Ibid., p. 480.
40. Ibid.
41. Ibid., pp. 480-481.
42. Ibid., p. 481.
43. Küng, The Church, p. 273.
44. McDonnell, Charismatic Renewal and Ecumenism, p. 70.
45. Ibid., p. 71.
46. Suenens, Ecumenism and Charismatic Renewal, p. 27.
47. Ibid., p. 4.
48. Ibid., pp. 4-5.
49. Theological and Pastoral Orientations, p. 7.
50. Ibid., p. 8.
51. Ibid.
52. Ibid., p. 11.
53. Ibid.
54. Ibid., p. 10.
55. Suenens, A New Pentecost?, p. 192.
56. Ibid., pp. 192-193.
57. Suenens, Ecumenism and Charismatic Renewal, p. 22.
58. Ratzinger, p. 73.
59. McDonnell, Charismatic Renewal and Ecumenism, p. 70.
60. Ibid., pp. 70-71.
61. Ibid.
62. Suenens, Ecumenism and Charismatic Renewal, p. 10.
63. Ibid., p. 11.
64. Ibid.
65. Suenens, Essays on Renewal, pp. 95-96.
66. Ibid., pp. 109-110.
67. Ibid., p. 110.
68. Ibid., p. 111.
69. Suenens, Ecumenism and Charismatic Renewal, p. 36.
70. Ibid., pp. 36-37.
71. Ibid., p. 36.
72. Ibid.
73. Ibid., p. 28.

74. Ibid., p. 27.
75. Ibid., p. 26.
76. Ibid., p. 27.
77. Wells, Revolution in Rome, p. 40.
78. Küng, Being a Christian, p. 495.
79. Ibid., p. 495.
80. Ibid., p. 496.
81. Ibid.
82. Küng, On Being a Christian, p. 496.
83. Ibid., p. 497.
84. Küng, Being a Christian, p. 498.
85. Ibid.
86. Ibid.

CHAPTER VI

CHARISMATIC RENEWAL AND MARIOLOGY

Having established the basic premise by
which the charismatic renewal will effect Catholicism,
namely, by emphasis on the trinitarian nature of the
movement and definition of the Church in mystical
categories, it remains to see how the renewal would
deal with specific problems which have created both
inward and outward divisions.

A foremost point of controversy would certainly be Mariology. Significantly, Vatican II
included Mariology in the schema on the Church
rather than in a separate chapter or subsuming it
under ecumenism. The result is an association of
Mary with the Church as representative of the nature
and mystery of the Church which de-emphasizes the
tension historically felt over her connection with
Christ as Redeemer.

Chapter eight, part II of Lumen Gentium
specifically addresses this latter question by
treating the role of Mary in the economy of salvation.
The office of the Mother is described as cooperative
and contributory to our salvation, but not in terms
which convey the idea of equality with Christ.[1]
The identity of Mary as established by tradition
is clearly stated (free from all stain of sin,
"fashioned" by the Holy Spirit into a kind of new
substance and a new creature) and her role defined
as one who, "in subordination to Him and along with
Him, by the grace of almighty God . . . served the
mystery of redemption." She is given a more
emphatic and official character by calling attention
to her earthly associations with Jesus (temple
dedication, Cana, the crucifixion) and, according
to tradition, her final assumption.[2]

In chapter III, "The Blessed Virgin and
the Church", the sole mediatorial office of Christ
is affirmed, with the mediatorial role of Mary
defined as a cooperative "sharing" in the priest-

hood of Christ.[3] The meaning of the Mother is as
a "model" for the Church which, while serving as
the ultimate example of "faith, charity and perfect
union" of the Church with Christ, at the same time
challenges the Church to become "herself a mother
by accepting God's word in faith."[4]

The Church, moreover, contemplating Mary's
mysterious sanctity, imitating her charity,
and faithfully fulfilling the Father's will,
becomes herself a mother by accepting God's
word in faith. For by her preaching and by
baptism she brings forth to a new and immortal
life children who are conceived of the Holy
Spirit and born of God. The Church herself is
a virgin, who keeps whole and pure the fidelity she has pledged to her Spouse. Imitating
the Mother of her Lord, and by the power of
the Holy Spirit, she preserves with virginal
purity an integral faith, a firm hope, and a
sincere charity.[5]

Concerning devotion to the blessed Mother,
the Council does not compromise concerning the cult
of adoration which has been part of Catholic history.
Such devotions are to be treasured as recommendations
by the teaching authority of the Church during the
course of centuries. At the same time, caution is
urged that theologians and preachers carefully avoid
"the falsity of exaggeration on the one hand, and
the excess of narrow-mindedness on the other."[6]

As with most doctrinal conflicts resulting
from tension between Scripture and tradition, the
Church seems merely to state the opposing views,
warn against exaggeration on either side and leave
the remaining problem without offering a direct
solution. While Protestants would react more favor-
ably to the integration of Mary with ecclesiology,
Catholics for some reason failed to realize a
revived Mariology as had been hoped. Indeed, it
has been generally recognized that the period after
the Council has been a time of "considerable
lessening of appreciation for Mary":

99

There was a reaction against a Marian theology
which was too essentialist, deductive, abstract,
and concentrated on her privileges in a context
that was not Christological. This reaction was
opposed to a Marian devotion that remained on
the edge of liturgical renewal, was too dependent upon private revelations, and too remote
from biblical theology. Besides, at the Council, a concern for ecumenism, which was always
in the thoughts of the Fathers, meant that
stress tended to be laid on what is common to
all Christians: expressions likely to give rise
to controversy were "played down."

All this has resulted in a climate which,
if not opposed to Mary, at least shows restraint
where she is concerned. And, as always when
there is a reaction, we have not been spared
exaggerations in the other direction.7

The charismatic renewal would seek to
minister to this need through emphasizing the relation of the Holy Spirit to Mary in a manner which
would elevate her stature in current Catholic
thought. It should be noted that from the perspective of the charismatic renewal, the question of
Mary relates more to internal harmony and cooperation than to ecumenism. Interestingly, the cult
of Mary seems to have been somewhat at odds with
the renewal. The feeling is that charismatic
emphasis on the Holy Spirit has de-emphasized, and
sometimes usurped, the role of Mary. A charismatic priest observes:

I have friends who are dedicated to the
Blessed Mother who look with fear and apprehension on those who are in the Charismatic
Movement and pray for the conversion of those
straying brethren. And there are sincere
people in the Charismatic Movement who think
that devotion to Mary detracts from the true
worship of God and has no place in the life
of the Spirit.

With a foot in both camps, I have been
pained to witness this needless antagonism.
Though it is not true that all charismatics

are opposed to Mary, and all Marian devotees
against the Charismatic Movement, there has
been much opposition due to mutual misunder-
standings.[8]

Suenens admits, "On the face of it, one might fear
that the accent placed on the Holy Spirit within
the Renewal, would lessen or cause people to forget
the role of Mary. All the more so when one remembers
that the classical Pentecostal tradition has not
been favorable to devotion to Mary."[9]

This dissension, plus the historic Protestant attitude toward Mary, produces a two-fold
response from the renewal. First, Catholics are
reminded of a strong association between Mary and
the Holy Spirit:

The Spirit who fills Mary is and will
always be, the Spirit of the Son. It is the
Spirit who "Christianized" Mary at a depth
beyond our understanding. She is the Christian par excellence, filled to overflowing with
the Spirit of Christ. In Mary, the Holy Spirit
has created his masterpiece: she is his pride,
his glory.[10]

The experience of Mary is described as "one of the
most precious gifts of the Spirit, . . . she is a
charism of the Spirit in person."[11]

The appeal here is to remove any tension
between the Spirit and Mary by making charismatic
renewal the stimulus which will provoke a revival
of Marian devotion. The charismatic renewal therefore presents itself as the means by which Mary can
be restored to her true perspective:

I think therefore that there is a real
need today, to stress again Mary's role in the
perspective of the Holy Spirit. I am con-
vinced that Marian devotion will come to life
in the proportion that is linked to the Holy
Spirit and lived under his guidance. Mary
will then appear as the one upon whom the

Spirit showered his graces, as the first
Christian, the first charismatic.[12]

Relative to objections of historical
Protestantism, a restored view of Mary is then projected (in a seemingly unreasonable or at least
unlikely manner!) as a basic tool of ecumenism.
Speaking at "the world council of theologians" held
in Brussels in 1970, Suenens stressed the bond
between Mary and ecumenism in terms of the magi who
found Christ by first coming to the Mother.[13]
Frankly, this seems to be wishful thinking. It is
demonstrative, however, of the fact that the charismatic renewal has no intention of de-emphasizing or
minimizing the role of Mary. Suenens, for example,
delivered the inaugural address at the first international congress of the "Ecumenical Society of the
Blessed Virgin Mary", a group founded by Martin
Gillett for the specific purpose of advancing
ecumenism through Marian theology and dialogue.[14]

The Charismatic position concerning Mary
illustrates that Catholics are not necessarily
interested in doing away with Catholic theology
because they have received a charismatic experience.
One does not sense a major move to de-emphasize
Mary or to in any way forsake her. Of course, it
is difficult to ascertain the true content of
popular religious experience. Charismatic Catholics
would certainly seem likely to limit Mary's role
in their devotions, specifically, because the Holy
Spirit seems to assume the position of adoration.
There is no hint of this, however, in official
writings. Neither is there any indication that
Mariology might be limited in favor of ecumenical
dialogue. The attitude of the renewal is to preserve her historic position and pay greater attention to intra-Church harmony and cooperation.

NOTES

1. Abbott, pp. 86-88.
2. Ibid., p. 88-89.
3. Ibid., pp. 91-92.
4. Ibid., pp. 92-93.
5. Ibid., p. 93.
6. Ibid., pp. 94-95.
7. Suenens, A New Pentecost?, pp. 196-197.
8. Louis Pfaller and Larry J. Alberts, Mary is Pentecostal. (pecos, New Mexico: Dove Publications, 1973), p. 5.
9. Suenens, A New Pentecost?, p. 210.
10. Ibid., pp. 205-206.
11. Ibid., p. 211.
12. Ibid., p. 197.
13. Ibid., p. 201
14. Ecumenism and Charismatic Renewal, p. 80, and A New Pentecost?, p. 200.

CHAPTER VII

The question of this section is whether
charismatic religious experience is truly congruent
with Catholic religious experience. An even larger,
but necessary question is how the charismatic movement should be evaluated in reference to the visible,
pluriform body of Christ.

The first question, naturally, contains
seeds for much criticism. Most immediate is the
question of whether the charismatic way of knowing
God is truly the Catholic way of knowing God. The
common ingredient in all charismatic renewal movements is the immediate personal awareness of God,
and the consequent assurance that comes from that
awareness. In the words of H. Dermot McDonald:

No "faith", scaffolded by "Five Ways" or
by five thousand, can bring this final personal
certainty. As long as religion is similar to
"knowledge about" it will remain open to doubt.
Arguments are as the scaffolding to the building,
they are not the building itself. All strictly
rational theology, be it scholastic or deistic,
which lacks the intimacy born of personal
immediate apprehension, cannot but have a certain
residue of uncertainty. It is precisely this
lack of certainty which, in the one case, has
brought about the claim for a papal infallibility and, in the other, to a personal one.[1]

Küng observes that all enthusiasts, from
pure Quakerism to social revolutionaries have in
common the idea of a direct working of the Spirit
which makes the Biblical message only conditionally
normative and possesses a revelation which goes
beyond Christ and the New Testament:

It is no small wonder that enthusiasts
of all periods have chosen to base their ideas
on John in particular. From these and similar
Johannine sayings they have concluded that the

Spirit teaches a particular wisdom which exceeds what Jesus said himself. They have claimed that the Spirit working in them has revealed the truth to them personally and directly. The revelation was direct in two senses, indicative of the opposition to them which took on different forms and emphasis in history: directly as opposed to a revelation which is fundamentally linked to the <u>word of Scripture</u>; and directly as opposed to a communication of the Spirit, which is supposed to come only through <u>ecclesiastical</u> office.[2]

One wonders whether the charismatic Catholic believer would not be living on two parallel tracks of religious experience, a visible series of "moments" accompanied by an invisible series of "moments." Where does certainty come from in the act of worship? From the eucharist or the inward witness of the Spirit? An unquestioned truth of Catholic theology is that office and charism are not opposed to each other, that Church and Spirit are in no way antithetical. The intention of Catholicism is that one should have a complete religious experience within the ordinary and established offices of the Church.

Yet, the charismatic renewal displays a type of experience that is extraneous to the elements of the Church. Are charismatics not worshipping when they are gathered in a prayer meeting? There is no problem in conventions and large meetings when priests and bishops are in attendance and the elements of Catholic worship are provided. But what of relations with the local parish? Where does worship take place in the ongoing parish life? Renewal in its present form seems to be leading away from the local parish rather than toward it. John Haughey makes the following penetrating critique:

There seems to be talk in the renewal about the renewal being oriented to and for the Church, taking place in the Church, and eventually disappearing. But there seems to be little preparation for what this means in practice. When is the task of charismatic leadership that of preparing for its own disappearance? If the

timing is not discerned accurately, the pre-
mature fadeaway of charismatic leadership can
leave the marriage between Christ and that
portion of his people affected by the renewal
precarious. On the other hand, when the fadeaway is overdue, the community that should have
been incorporated into the structural life of
the Church remains ectopically positioned in
the Body of Christ, unable to vitalize the
Body or be vitalized by it.[3]

Haughey cautions charismatic leaders to
remember that "Roman Catholics cannot bind themselves forever to a community in the Body of Christ
that intends to leave forever indeterminate its own
relationship to the visible, social, institutional
reality in that Body which is the Roman Catholic
Church."[4]

The above, however, is still more of a
question than an answer. The problem still remains
of how to relate inward charismatic experience to
the Church without violating the primacy of the
latter. For this possible tension to be resolved,
it it necessary to search for the reason why the
spiritual elements of religion have often seemed
at odds with the visible elements of religion.
Indeed, upon leaving the Church of Acts, history
seems to show no ideal example of such a wedding.
Perhaps the greatest error is to assume that history contains a "model" of the Church which will
solve for us all the problems of religious experience. The ancient Church contended with the heresy
of Montanism. The Church of the Middle Ages
experienced great conflict over the teachings of
Joachim of Flora and his successors, many of whom
are the ancestors of pietistic movements today.
Protestant Churches fared no better; only by vio-
lence was Luther able to deal with the enthusiasts.
The Counter-Reformation Church without the Scripture
and the post-Reformation Church with Scripture both
evidenced the same tensions.

The source of the problem is not historical or governmental--it is theological. Charismatic experience has been generally destructive to the Church because it contains a definition and view of the Holy Spirit alien to the Church. The hint of the problem comes from the tension felt by those who adore Mary. Why would some of these perceive the charismatic renewal as a threat? Is it not because the renewalists seemed to make the Holy Spirit an object of devotion in competition with Mary? The Holy Spirit assumes a cultic status which makes Him the third element in a type of scholastic "higher mathematics" concerning the Trinity. To be sure, this tendency is not immediately evident from official writings; perhaps the charismatics themselves are not really aware of the emphasis. The entire framework of Catholic experience, however, would make room for such an application. The adoration of Mary, numerous saints, and the tendency to create "objects" such as relics for worship displays a type of thinking that would easily make such a transition.

Whenever the Spirit is assigned a role which violates the economic and revelatory relationship within the Trinity, tension will invariably develop between the Son and the Spirit. The Holy Spirit is the Spirit of Christ (II Cor. 3:18; Ga. 4:6; Ro. 8:9; Ph. 1:19 and I Cor. 15:45) just as he is the third person of the Trinity (II Cor. 3:13; I Cor. 12:4-6; Ga. 4:4-6; Rom. 5:1-5). The proper relation of these two facts is critical for religious experience. There seems to be a "popular tritheism" in Christianity which views the Spirit as an added God or a "third party" in divine-human relationships. Practically applied, such distortion leads to a role of the Spirit which is revelatory in a gnostic sense rather than Hebrew-Christian. Küng states:

> The Spirit is no other than God _himself_: God close to man and the world, as comprehending but not comprehensible, self-bestowing but not controllable, life-giving but also direc-

tive power and force. He is then not a third
party, not a thing between God and men, but
God's personal closeness to men. Most mis-
understandings of the Holy Spirit arise from
setting him apart from God mythologically and
making him independent. In this respect the
Council of Constantinople itself in 381, to
which we owe the extension of the Nicene Creed
to include the Holy Spirit, expressly emphasizes
the fact that the Spirit is of one nature with
the Father and the Son.[5]

Charismatic movements seem not to understand
such unity of nature, nor the practical applications
contained therein. Joachim of Flora, in his projection of a "third age of the Holy Spirit", portrays
a basically Hegelian concept of Spirit as higher
revelation with his generation, of course, being the
ultimate fulfillment of God's plan.[6]

The tension seems to come from viewing the
Spirit dialectically, as the "next step", "the
higher revelation", the "secret" of God. The
function of the Spirit in such a framework is to
bring visions, prophecies, to "add to" and "supplement" both God's word and God's Son. The Holy Spirit
viewed in such a framework means that Jesus is not
enough, God the Father is not enough, that only
when the "third ingredient" is added can one have a
complete religious experience.

Where the tension comes from is difficult
to say. Perhaps there was an overemphasis on the
speculative language of the Cappadocians, resulting,
as Küng would say, in a type of higher trinitarian
mathematics.[7] Perhaps the doctrine of the procession
of the Spirit was not sufficiently clarified, or
too soon forgotten. At any rate, a view of the
Spirit is current which seems to violate his revelatory office and personal identity in favor of a
Hegelian-like process. Overemphasizing the term
"person" in the Trinity gives birth to a dialec-
ticism if not tritheism.

109

A view of the office and function of the
Spirit more congruent with Catholic aims is presented by Yves Congar. The Holy Ghost, he says,
is the "active priciple" which enables human efforts
to realize "the history of salvation."[8]

In all this the Holy Ghost is not acting
personally, in the sense that his work is new
or different from Christ's; he realizes and
gives an inner depth to what was said and done
once and for all by Christ, which is the Gospel
(cf. John 14:26; 16:12-13). The grace and
truth of the Gospel has been fixed once for
all, at least with regard to its essential
features, in the historical and visible mission
of the incarnate Word, that is, by Jesus Christ;
the Gospel determines the structure of the new
and eternal covenant; it is useless to expect
or create other forms. This unique and particular event, which is nevertheless accessible to
all times, and which must be spread throughout
the world and through history, being applied
to an infinite variety of people and situations
is an essential feature of the economy of salvation. The special task of the Spirit is to
ensure from within that many different people
down the centuries and scattered over the sur-
face of the globe share in this form of truth
and life. He is able to do this, being "Spirit",
that is, a presence that is etheral and not
bound by frontiers, at the same time universal
and interior. But since he is the Spirit of
Christ his work is Christ's; he simply realizes
and infuses his personality into the Gospel
form of saving truth and life laid down and
instituted on earth by Christ, who watches over
its accomplishment, seated henceforward "at
the right hand of the Father." By the Spirit
this institution becomes thus a perpetual
"event", present and active. There is a meeting
and union between a present action by God that
is immediate and vertical so to speak, and the
transmission of the framework of the covenant
by an historical and visible succession, which
is horizontal as it were: in exactly the same
way that in a personal act of faith, the external

110

communication of defined truths effected by a
visible succession of ministers (who after
Christ form a single missionary body) meets
and fuses with an inspiration or spiritual force
that is received immediately and "vertically"
from God in the innermost depths of our hearts.[9]

The proper view of the Spirit, then, is as
a dynamic principle constantly applying the unified
plan of salvation. The Holy Spirit is not to "press
beyond" God's revelation in Christ, it is not to
"supplement" so that either the Father or the Son
come to be seen as inferior, inadequate, or incomplete.
The true Catholic way of viewing the Spirit, according
to Congar, is rather the category of "bearing witness."[10]
The Spirit affirms the truth of Scripture, the command-
ments of God and the proclamation of Jesus Christ.[11]
Although Protestants might disagree concerning the
application of such operations to tradition (hence
the difficulties of Vatican II), still the direction
is correct. The Spirit as witness always looks
toward Christ, never beyond him or away from him.

Donald Gelpi senses this possible difficulty
when he observes:

To the extent, therefore, that the charismatic experience has derived its theological
interpretation exclusively from the trinitarian
polemics of the Fathers, it has tended to regard
the triune God as the transcendent object of
worship rather than as a saving presence within
history guiding the salvific destinies of men.
In other words, while the Subordinationists
had not succeeded in forcing the orthodox to a
denial of the divinity of either the Son or
the Spirit, the heretics had succeeded in introducing into the Christian experience a feeling
for the divine transcendence which suggested
certain aspects of Subordinationist piety.

The shifting mood of popular piety was
reflected in the worship of the Christian
community from the fifth century on. Until
the Arian crisis, Christians had prayed to the

111

Father through the Son in the Spirit. Their
piety was, therefore, involved with the sense
that there is a unique salvific relationship
binding the community to each of the divine
Persons. But in the face of the Arian taunt
that to pray "through the Son and in the
Spirit" implied a Subordinationist theology,
orthodox piety began to insist on giving equal
worship to each of the divine Persons. Prayers
to Christ, to the Spirit and to the Blessed
Trinity became more common. They were, in
effect, a popular repudiation of anything that
smacked of heretical Subordinationism.[12]

Granted that this reflects a certain historical
context, the fact remains that Catholic devotional
life with its multiple adorations and objects of
devotion can lend itself more easily than most to a
distorted view of the function and nature of the
Spirit.

          The solution for the future may be in a
revival of the filoque, a more clear or emphasized
statement of the work and relationship of the
Spirit. Of course such an emphasis would not do
a great deal for relations with the Eastern Church.
A risky but possibly acceptable solution would be
an emphasis upon the trinity as a "revelational
unity" as advanced by Kung.[13] This would involve
maintaining the classical trinitarian theology, but
emphasizing the Spirit as the presence of "God and
the exalted Christ" in both the community and the
individual believer. Kung's intention is to
emphasize the unity of God's divine nature rather
than the triplicity of persons. One would see the
Trinity, therefore, as the functionally progressive
revelation of God to man with the Spirit being the
presence of God in the individual believer.
"Spirit" would be the sphere in which Jesus moves
in our midst, "the Spirit of God. . .understood
also as the Spirit of Jesus as exalted to God."[14]
By stressing the unity of God's nature, one would
seem to provide a corrective for charismatic
excesses. Such a course is only safe with constant

reminders that each member of the revelational Trinity is a person in the best Cappadocian sense and that modalism is no option. Simply, each member of the Trinity must be seen as the personal presence of God.

The charismatic renewal may and hopefully will respond to this question by defining their movement and destiny in a manner which reflects "bearing witness" to the work of Christ and his body the Church. Confusion results when charismatic authority misinterprets its nature or attempts to influence behavior outside of this context. The renewal must present the posture of "looking toward" Christ by preparing to disappear as salt bringing savor to the whole body. To the extent that the renewal does not disappear, but perpetuates itself with its own leadership, communities and worship, to that extent it is liable to look away from the center of the Church and thus follow the path of enthusiasm.

NOTES

1. H. Dermot McDonald, What is meant by Religious Experience?", Vox Evangelica, 1963 Edition, London Bible College, p. 68.
2. Küng, The Church, pp. 191-192.
3. Theological Reflections on the Charismatic Renewal, pp. 109-110.
4. Ibid., p. 111.
5. Küng, Being a Christian, pp. 469-470.
6. Küng, The Church, p. 195.
7. Küng, On Being a Christian, p. 474.
8. Yves Congar, The Meaning of Tradition, pp. 52-53.
9. Ibid., pp. 53-54.
10. Ibid., pp. 52-53.
11. Ibid.
12. Küng, On Being a Christian, pp. 472 ff.
13. Ibid., pp. 476-477.
14. Ibid., p. 470.

CHAPTER VIII

CONCLUSION

Kevin Ranaghan notes that the charismatic renewal centers in three key areas: (1) personal conversion, (2) radical discipleship and (3) being "gather together" in corporate worship and sharing.[1]

The first of these, personal conversion, means the establishment of a deep personal relationship with God. This is accomplished by "turning our lives over to Him as completely as we are capable of doing."[2] The terminology here is identical to that of American revivalism; God is calling the Church to a primary life of worship and praise in which the death and resurrection of Christ is accepted as the very center of one's life.

The concept of radical discipleship involves a "following in Christ's footsteps." The idea is that of being "enabled" or "empowered" for service, best conveyed by the term "baptism in the Holy Spirit."

The concept of being "gathered together" is primary for all who have been baptized in the Spirit. "Just as the experience of the first Pentecost led the three thousand to come together in the life of the primitive community, so too, there is a communal, a group aspect to the charismatic renewal wherever it is manifested."[3] Charismatics feel that through the renewal, God is calling His people all over the world together to a life of corporate witness, sharing and service to the Church and the world.

Utilizing these three areas as a way of schematizing the charismatic renewal, one may make the following evaluation. First, the thrust of personal conversion is said to bring new life to worship. Catholics testify to a new expectancy toward the sacraments and a new appreciation of

115

their importance. Each seems to become a more
personal experience. One has to question, however,
whether grace is really operating in a Catholic
manner. Catholic sacraments convey grace, spiritual
benefits being applied to participants through them.
Charismatics, however, seem to see grace as existentially realized from within. One might say that
charismatics come to worship "bringing their grace
with them." There is agreement concerning the nature
of grace, but seeming contradiction concerning the
operation of grace. Although there is no logical
or theological reason charismatic worshippers could
not adapt to sacramental structures, sacramental and
charismatic worship have not been joined at the broad
local level. "Baptism in the Spirit" has not been
successfully integrated with sacramental baptism,
confirmation and the eucharist.

     The second central concern of the renewal,
radical discipleship, relates to definition of charisms
as well as charismatic communities. Vatican II
certainly allows for a view of charisms as more
spontaneous, emotive and alive than pre-Vatican II
definitions. The latter sound more like philosophical categories than gifts of service or power. In
Catholic theology, however, it is the Church that is
charismatic rather than the individual. There is a
charismatic element "in the Church" as it interprets,
validates and applies spiritual truths. Can the
individualistic and subjective emphasis of renewalists
merge harmoniously with the more institutional concepts? Historically, movements which have been dis-
tinguished by gifts of preternatural endowments have
become ultimately divisive. Either the Church found
them unacceptable or they rejected the Church. It
is not a healthy sign that the majority of charismatic manifestations such as prophecy, healings and
tongues are taking place outside the local parish
in prayer meetings and charismatic conventions.
No matter how large the prayer meeting or convention,
the Church has not been charismatically renewed
until renewal objectives have been realized in the
local parish. The renewal must be brought to the
Church, not the Church to the renewal!

116

The same is true of communities. The Church is intended to provide the same contributions as community/life, as adherents would readily admit. Yet there has been no significant integration of this life-style into the local parish or the Church at large. There seems to be no reason why the communities which continue will not follow the same pattern as the Brudherhof, developing a separate social and religious identity within the parent institution. They seem to be spiritually, socially and philosophically alien to normative Roman Catholicism.

The third central concern of the renewal, the concept of "being gathered together", involves both a positive and speculative consideration. Positively, the renewal shines in its zeal for the ecumenical purpose of the Church. Vatican II images of the Church as a "people on the way", of its spiritual and mysterious constitution and charismatic authority are synonymous with charismatic viewpoints. Renewalists see themselves as fulfilling Pope Paul's pneumatological sketch of the Church as fulfillment of the Day of Pentecost. But a problem still remains, again, in relating these eclectic groups to the visible authority structures of the Church. The unity displayed by the renewal so far seems to be primarily nondenominational rather than ecumenical. The question is whether unity based on charismatic experience can preserve the dialectical quality of ecumenism.

The Catholic Church recognizes the necessity of disagreement, but does the charismatic laity? Such a necessity would be very difficult to prove to an ardent worshipper who weekly prays and sings with Christians of other faiths. There is danger that charismatic Catholics will view the Church as moving too slowly toward a goal which they feel is just over the horizon. This could and has led some to join Protestant charismatic Churches. Charismatics follow their religious experience and woe be to any Church which does not maintain an environment conducive to that experience. The Catholic Church is still on probation, the renewal

being too young to yet interpret its destiny within
the Church. Should, however, the Church not continue to respond, the charismatics will follow
their experience wherever it leads them.

At the same time, it might not pay to be
overly generous. Vatican II boldly recognized the
existence of other "Churches", thus establishing a
theological identity for them. The charismatic
renewal supplements this theological ideal by
supplying a common religious experience. Both
elements create an atmosphere which could lead to
serious loss of Catholic adherents. The sacraments
by themselves may not be strong enough to hold the
constituency. The Church faces a delemma--if it
remains too conservative, it will lose members; if
it is too symphathetic, the same thing will happen.

The question remains whether the renewal is
truly a "break-through" in evangelical terms of
crisis commitment. The answer is "yes" if one
speaks in terms of Catholics who testify to a revitalized or new faith in Christ. The answer is "no"
if one defines renewal as any change in distinctive
Catholic doctrine. Individuals have experienced
charismatic renewal, but the Church has not yet been
charismatically renewed.

This is not to say that the renewal is
antagonistic toward the Church, or, aside from some
negative initial impressions, that the Church is
hostile to the renewal. Predictions of persecution
or repression such as David Wilkerson's The Vision
have simply not come to pass. Neither has the
charismatic testimony resulted in factionalism
which has so often been the curse of the movement
in Protestant circles.

Rather, one senses a deeper tension between
opposing external and internal religious systems.
After Augustine the Church seems to have divided
into two opposing theological systems--the rational
and the experential. In the first, reason led to
faith with the thought of Aquinas usurping that of

Augustine until the time of the Reformation. In the latter, experience led to faith with numerous charismatic groups maintaining experential options, often at odds with the confessional majority.

Given the distinctive structure of Catholic doctrine, it is difficult to see how the renewal can avoid this historical conflict. Renewal of any type is only as effective as the view of revelation and authority upon which it stands. For Catholics, this means an apologetical and theological system which by its very nature contends with charismatic renewal, making it an auxillary path to God rather than a complement to the faith historically held by the Church.

Perhaps the most evident fact about the renewal is that it has not been absorbed into the Church. If anything it has gone in the other direction, constantly multiphying its forms and solidfying an identity apart from the Church. The renewal is just entering its second decade and it is during this time that goals should begin to be achieved. Now is a very critical period for the renewal; hoped-for objectives should be visible in embryo. For the renewal to continue to be taken seriously there must be some ascertainable success within the visible Church in the very near future.

Regardless of the eventual outcome, the renewal has confronted the Church in a positive and challenging manner by questioning the content of Catholic religious experience. The zealous faith evidenced by thousands of charismatics is a sober reminder to Catholics and Protestants both that spiritual renewal can never be less than spiritual--that the "rushing wind" can never be confined to the dogmas men think or contained in the vessels they create.

APPENDIX

INTERVIEWS

Interview with Ralph Martin by James Breckenridge -
May 29, 1976, South Bend, Indiana.

Question:

Do you have any comments on the significance of the
Catholic Charismatic Movement for potential Eastern-
Western union?

Answer:

I think that the Greek Orthodox for a long time have
felt that the Western Church, the Roman Church, has
become somewhat sort of legalized and formalized and
theologized and that way they sort of left off a
living experience with the Holy Spirit. I think that
the overall experience people are having, the sense
they are having, is that awakening the Roman Church
to a more mystical life or a greater role of the
Holy Spirit in the Church is going to make it more
possible for union with the Orthodox who have always
had a sense of the working of the Spirit or of more
worship and adoration, that type of thing, than the
Roman Church has had. So I think that what's
happening is that charismatic renewal is sort of
making up for some deficiencies in the spiritual
life or worship in the Roman Church that is going
to help with reunion. I think that just the more
the Holy Spirit is free to work in both branches of
the Church, the more we are going to be able to come
into one mind and one heart. I can't say that it
is doing anything but helping reunion.

Question:

How would you differentiate between, or what is the
difference between, the Catholic Charismatic Renewal
now and its manifestations and development, and the

development and manifestations of the Jansenists and Camisards and the various other groups covered by Ronald Knox in his book entitled Enthusiasm?

Answer:

The one difference is that from the very beginning this renewal has planted itself firmly within the existing ecclesiastical authority and jurisdiction (and) has never claimed to be an independent source of discernment or guidance but has always claimed to be under and submitted to the existing majesterium of the Church, and so practically speaking the renewal has grown up everywhere in the Church and from the very beginning made that explicit kind of choice, recognizing the dangers that beset renewal movements of becoming schismatic. That is not what God is doing; that is not what we choose. We choose this to be a renewal within the Church from the very beginning, explicitly submitting it to the authority of the bishops.

Question:

Dr. Josephine Ford, in Which Way for Catholic Pentecostals?, maintains that there are actually two types of Catholic charismatics in the Catholic Church. The first group is a more fluid, loosely defined group as opposed to your seemingly more authoritarian National Charismatic Committee. She would feel that the structured, ecclesiastisized organized body of the renewal is not preserving or advancing the true interests of charismatic renewal. Do you feel this thesis is at all valid?

Answer:

It is hard for me to take too seriously what Dr. Ford says because what I think is at the root of this whole problem, is right here in the early days of the charismatic renewal in South Bend. She walked into a prayer meeting and said, "I have a doctorate in Scripture; I should run the meeting!" The people said, "We don't believe that just because

you have a doctorate in Scripture you should run
the meeting." From then on she has been conducting
this running warfare with the leadership here in
South Bend. I think, as a matter of fact, there is
a real diversity on the National Service Committee.
You have Dr. Harold Cohen, who isn't part of a
covenant community, has never been part of a covenant community, as representative of sort of the
average sort of development of the charismatic
renewal in the average parish, you know, not cummu-
nity-oriented. You have Father Mike Scanlon, who
basically comes out of the same background, you
know, who is running a college and goes around
preaching and talking--I think her view of two
types is a very simplistic, I think that what she
is trying to say is that there is a good type that
she likes and a bad type that she doesn't like.
I think its sort of that kind of thing. It is
really hard for me to take seriously what she is
saying.

Question:

Can you in any way equivocate charismatic renewal
with the community movement; that if one is a
Catholic charismatic, one would ipso facto be
associated with a covenant community?

Answer:

Community living is sort of a logical unfolding of
the charismatic renewal, but it isn't like an
essential link. A lot of people get a taste of the
charismatic renewal and would like to leave it
there as a taste. Others feel it is the beginning
of a normal progression. We are not saying that
everybody should be part of a covenant community.
It's a helpful thing but I wouldn't say it's the
right thing in every situation. That may not be
what the Lord's doing in a particular situation.
The material or ingredients for a solid community
may not exist, and it may be more helpful to have
another kind of relationship.

Question:

Is the "discipling" controversy current in some
Protestant Churches similar to problems the renewal
might face in its relations with the Catholic Church?

Answer:

I think the questioning of "discipling" was more of
a controversy in Protestant sectors of the charismatic renewal than in the Catholic movement.
Authority and obedience relationships have always
been a part of the Catholic tradition. It's no
big deal, that's how the Catholic Church works.
The real stir that was being caused was that some
of the more free-wheeling, independent Protestant
pentecostals were beginning to talk about the needs
of submission and authority and community, and that
was causing a tremendous shock wave in the free-
wheeling, independent, "nobody's my Pope, nobody's
going to tell me what to do, I'm going to start my
own Church" mentality within independent, fragmenting
American Protestantism. There was a strong reaction
from that segment; some of them even charged their
own members with espousing a "return to Rome."
It's not really been a problem within the Catholic
charismatic renewal.

Interview with Karl Rahner by James Breckenridge -
November 7, 1974, Jesuit Retreat House, Chicago,
Illinois.

<u>Question</u>:

At the recent Catholic Charismatic Convention at
Notre Dame University (June 14-16, 1974), the
feeling was expressed strongly that this movement
represents a tremendous upheaval or spiritual revival
in the Catholic Church. Donald Gelpi, for example,
says:

> Pope Paul's recent proclamation of a Holy Year
> of Pentecost in order to effect the "charis-
> matic" renewal of the entire church, can scarcely
> have been purely coincidental with the growth
> of the international movement of piety. The
> Holy Father is certainly well aware of the
> charismatic renewal. Indeed, his earlier
> cautionary remarks about potential problems in
> the renewal make full sense in the light of his
> Holy Year proclamation.[1]

Fr. Gelpi then proceeds to quote for further support
Pope John's convocation from the Second Vatican
Council:

> Renew your wonders in our time, as though
> for a new Pentecost, and grant that the holy
> Church, preserving unanimous and continuous
> prayer, together with Mary, the mother of Jesus,
> and also under the guidance of St. Peter, may
> increase the reign of the Divine Savior, the
> reign of truth and justice, the reign of love
> and peace. Amen.[2]

My question is: is it legitimate for the Catholic
charismatics to claim this much support from the
Holy Father?

<u>Answer</u>:

First of all, the Pope also made some very
<u>cautious</u> statements about the Roman group and,
secondly, what the Pope says should be identified
with the charismatic movement in that narrower
sense so that the Pope's statement in that regard

125

as applied to the entire charismatic renewal movement would be very questionable theologically. Theology has all sorts of norms for weighing these Papal statements and that would have to be applied in this situation, how important it was and so on. (For example,) the Popes on social questions have spoken with much more authority and solemnity, in encyclicals say, and this has not really had much effect, although perhaps their statements should have. So, if you just take this one address of the Pope, it has to be weighed against many more important or solemn declarations. Perhaps Suenens, the Cardinal of Brussels, had some influence on this particular address. That doesn't make it wrong! You have to be careful not to give more weight to that Papal statement than the Pope gave to it or intended to give to it.

Question:

Is it legitimate for the Catholic charismatic movement to call itself a "renewal" within the Church in the sense that they are renewing the original faith of the Catholic Church?

Answer:

The have exactly as much right to make that claim as the arguments and evidence they give to support it. And secondly, their justification cannot just come from some scriptural text in the New Testament, but whether or not our present situation is calling for precisely this kind of movement. Even if it did perhaps work in the past, you cannot just transport that from out of the past into the present. Therefore, their arguments and their evidence depends not only on the New Testament, but on the concrete effect they are having on the contemporary situation.

Question:

Is the charismatic renewal merely transitory?

Answer:

If you will get the history of the Church, there are always these renewal movements, the Monks, the

126

Franciscans, the sixteenth century Jesuits; these always, at the moment, tend to overvalue themselves. They see themselves as the renewal of the Church. But if you look at the Franciscans, how they looked upon themselves as the "new light" or the "final reform" of the Church, but in time you see how it was limited; or the Jesuits in their work in the Counter-Reformation--there was a positive thing, but nevertheless, there were all sorts of other things going on, so at the moment there is this tendency to overvalue for the Church the importance of the movement, but in time one can see its limitations.

Question:

James Hitchock wrote a book which was very critical of the results of the Second Vatican Council (The Decline and Fall of Radical Catholicism. New York: Herder and Herder, 1971). It is his thesis that the Council has failed because of a number of things, e.g., lassitude, neglect, etc. I asked Cardinal Suenens at the Notre Dame conference whether he felt that perhaps the charismatic movement was the thing which was going to bring all the churches together. It was his opinion that this is indeed the case--that the renewal will be a strong element in eventually uniting all the churches. The Charismatics seem to feel that their movement is going to do what Vatican II failed to do, thereby bringing about the hoped-for reforms.

Answer: (Rahner answers in three parts)

First, insofar as the charismatic movement is striving for genuine religious experience, contact with the Spirit and so on, that is a good thing and we have too little of that in the Church and so in general that is a good movement.

    However, with regard to uniting the Churches, the segments of the population that it is touching is very limited, a small part and therefore even should they be successful here, what effect will

127

that have on the total population of the churches? So it is questionable, however successful they are within these limited segments, whether or not in that sense (they are correct). Their tendency is to over-estimate their own value because they are working within a very limited segment of the church population.

Secondly, perhaps they are too little in touch with what would be psychological reflections upon the nature of these experiences and also say, reflections that would come from the history of the Church where this type of thing has been going on; that is to say, the evaluation of the religious depth of the experience perhaps would have to encounter psychological evaluations of what is going on.

Thirdly, perhaps they are not in close enough touch with the spiritual history of the Church or the history of spiritual experience in the Church; can they tie themselves into, say, the history of mysticism--spirituality in the Church? Perhaps they have not done that enough.

There is a long history in the Church of the critical evaluation of mystical experiences and they have not done enough of that with regard to their own experience to evaluate, criticize and discern the value of a lot of this history. For example, the gift of tongues--I would not deny that this could have a good effect or bear good fruit, but then the real value can also be over-estimated. And then in the other examples, say, in the so-called cures, in the miraculous sense of sickness and so on, the Church has very well-established norms for judging whether or not there was a real cure here. Has the charismatic movement applied these very strict norms to what they are calling miraculous cures and healings? Should they (for example) take the norms that are used at Lourdes or the norms that exist in canonization processes and so on? Perhaps there would be fewer things that would be able to be called cures than they are calling miraculous cures.

I have nothing against sudden conversions or the baptism of the Spirit, but looking at this from the history of the Church and so on, that has to be a sudden, momentary conversion when really understood can be seen as the fruit or the effect of a very long, long process.

Question:

You do accept the fact that there could be such a thing as speaking in tongues?

Answer:

(Certainly) it can happen, but whether that comes from the Holy Spirit is another question. Much, say, with regard to the gift of tongues can be explained from psychological realms. What are the real motives or the real grounds underneath the phenomenon? All the same phenomena can be found outside the Christian world and they fit right into the same type psychological structure as our own fit and therefore perhaps can be explained psychologically.

Question:

If the Catholic Christian receives the Spirit sacramentally but then at a later date, according to the charismatics, receives a fulfilling or outgrowth which enables him to exercise exceptional spiritual gifts, usually witnessed at private gatherings or prayer meetings, will this not lead to a "spiritual elitism" within the Church?

Answer:

This question of the relationship between sacramental reception and then the actualization, existential realization goes all the way back to Origen, the difference between the pneumatics and the Pseukikoi. This problem goes all the way back to the history of the Church and it is certainly true that simply the reception of a sacrament is not

necessarily the existential realization, actualization
in life, of what the grace of that sacrament is all
about. But there has been much said about this
question in the history of theology which the charismatics do not seem to be aware of and are not applying in their own situation.

Question:

But is there not a danger, speaking of this elitism,
that it could lead to a de-emphasis of the importance
of the priesthood?

Answer:

That could be a danger, and not necessarily is a
danger, but there are two dangers on two extremes.
One would be to so overvalue the objective order of
the sacraments that you neglect the need for the
subjective dispositions, reception, actualization,
and so on. Then the other extreme, which is the
danger you are talking about here, (is) to so over-
estimate in that sense the experience of grace that
you would simply take any value away from the whole
objective order of the sacraments. There is a
danger that either pole can be so stressed that the
other pole is lost sight of.

    Already in the Council of Ephesus, which was
something like 431, the Messalians were condemned.
(To them) the experience of grace was what mattered
and not the objective reception of the sacrament
of baptism, and so in many ways the charismatics
think that all these problems are new buth they're
really 1500 years old. At the time of Luther it
was the same type of problematic. He assumed that
the experience of justification was identified with
justification. The Counter-Reformation Catholic
side was that you need not just, in that sense,
subjective experience of, but also the objective
order of, sacraments. The two dangers are to over-
estimate either of the two sides, to identify
either the objective or subjective with the total
reality.

NOTES

1. Donald Gelpi, "Charismatic Renewal: Problems,
   Possibilities," National Catholic Reporter,
   Aug. 3, 1973, p. 7.
2. Documents of Vatican II, p. 709.

SOURCES CONSULTED

Books

Abbot, Walter, ed. The Documents of Vatican II.
    Translated by Joseph Gallagher. New York:
    Guild Press, 1966.

Barry, J. Colman, ed. Readings in Church History.
    Westminister, Md.: Newman Press, 1965

Berkouwer, G.C. Recent Developments in Roman
    Catholic Thought. Translated by J.J. Lamberts.
    Grand Rapids: Wm. B. Eerdmans Pub., Co., 1965.

_____. The Second Vatican Council and the New
    Catholicism. Translated by Lewis B. Smedes.
    Grand Rapids: Wm. B. Eerdmans Pub., Co., 1965.

Bittlinger, Arnold. Gifts and Ministries. Grand
    Rapids: Wm. B. Eerdmans Pub. Co., 1973.

_____. Gifts and Graces. Grand Rapids: Wm. B.
    Eerdmans Pub. Co., 1967.

Bromily, G.W. The Unity and Disunity of the Church.
    Grand Rapids: Wm. B. Eerdmans Pub. Co., 1958.

Brumback, Carl. What Meaneth This? Springfield:
    Gospel Pub. House, 1947.

Bruner, Frederick Dale. A Theology of the Holy
    Spirit. Grand Rapids: Wm. B. Eerdmans Pub.
    Co., 1970.

Byrne, James. Threshold of God's Promise. Notre
    Dame, Inc.: Ave Maria Press, 1970.

Clark, Stephen B. Building Christian Communities.
    Notre Dame, Ind: Ave Maria Press, 1972.

_____. Unordained Elders and Renewal Communities.
    New York: Paulist Press, 1976.

133

_____. _Where Are We Headed?_ Notre Dame, Ind.:
Charismatic Renewal Services, 1973.

Cleobsch, William Anthone. "Communities and Orders:
Protestant." _Twentieth Century Encyclopedia
of Religious Knowledge_. Grand Rapids: Baker
Book House, 1955. 1:278.

Congar, Yves. _The Meaning of Tradition_. Translated
by A.N. Woodrow. New York: Hawthorn Books,
1964.

Cullman, Oscar. _Vatican Council II: The New Direction_.
New York: Harper & Row, 1968.

Davis, Charles. _Theology for Today_. New York: Sheed
& Ward, 1962.

Fichter, Joseph H. _The Catholic Cult of the Paraclete_.
New York: Sheed & Ward, 1975.

Ford, J. Massyngberde. _Baptism of the Spirit_. Techny,
Ill.: Divine Word Pub., 1971.

_____. _Which Way for Catholic Pentecostals?_
New York: Harper & Row, 1976.

Freemantle, Anne, ed. _The Papal Encyclicals in their
Historical Context_. New York: New American
Library, 1963.

Frost, Robert C. _Aglow With The Spirit_. Plainfield,
N.J.: Logos International, 1965.

Gee, Donald. _Concerning Spiritual Gifts_. Springfield,
Mo.: Gospel Pub. Hse., 1972.

Gelpi, Donald L. _Pentecostal Piety_. New York: Paulist
Press, 1972.

_____. _Pentecostalism: A Theological Viewpoint_.
New York: Paulist Press, 1971.

134

Greeley, Andrew M. The American Catholic: A Social
    Portrait. New York: Basic Books, 1977.

Hanu, Jose. Vatican Encounter: Conversations With
    Archbishop Marcel Lefebvre. Kansas City:
    Sheed Andrews & McMeel, 1978.

Hardon, John A. The Catholic Catechism. New York:
    Doubleday & Co., 1975.

Hitchcock, James. The Decline and Fall of Radical
    Catholicism. New York: Image Books, 1971.

Hollenweger, Walter J. The Pentecostals. Minneapolis:
    Augsburg Pub. Hse., 1972.

Hughes, Ray H. What is Pentecost? Cleveland, Tenn.:
    Pathway Press, 1963.

International Directory of Catholic Charismatic
    Prayer Groups. South Bend, Ind.: Charismatic
    Renewal Services, 1975.

Kildahl, John P. The Psychology of Speaking in
    Tongues. New York: Harper & Row, 1972.

Killgallon, James and Weber, Gerard. Life in Christ:
    Instructions in the Catholic Faith. Chicago:
    Life in Christ, 1958.

Kosicki, George W. The Lord Is My Shepherd. Ann
    Arbor: Charismatic Renewal Services, 1973.

Kung, Hans. On Being a Christian. Translated by
    Edward Quinn. New York: Pocket Books, 1978.

_____. The Church. New York: Sheed & Ward, 1967.

Latourette, Kenneth Scott. A History of Christianity.
    New York: Harper & Row, 1953.

Manuel, David. Like a Mighty River. Orleans, Mass.:
    Rock Harbor Press, 1977.

Martin, George. Parish Renewal: A Charismatic
    Approach. Ann Arbor, Mich.: Word of Life, 1976.

135

Martin, Ralph. Fire on the Earth. Ann Arbor, Mich.:
    Word of Life, 1975.

_____. Unless the Lord Build the House. Notre
    Dame, Ind.: Ave Maria Press, 1971.

McDonnell, Kilian. The Charismatic Renewal and
    Ecumenism. New York: Paulist Press, 1978.

_____. ed. The Holy Spirit and Power: The
    Catholic Charismatic Renewal. New York:
    Doubleday & Co., 1975.

Muhlen Heribert. A Charismatic Theology: Initiation
    in the Spirit. Translated by Edward Quinn
    and Thomas Linton. London: Burns & Oates, 1978.

O'Brien, David J. The Renewal of American Catholicism.
    New York: Oxford University Press, 1972.

O'Connor, Edward D. "The Hidden Roots of the Charis-
    matic Renewal in the Catholic Church."
    Aspects of Pentecostal-Charismatic Origins.
    Edited by Vinson Synan. Plainfield, N.J.:
    Logos International, 1975.

_____. Pentecost in the Modern World. Notre Dame,
    Ind.: Ave Maria Press, 1972.

_____. The Pentecostal Movement in the Catholic
    Church. Notre Dame, Ind.: Ave Maria Press, 1971.

O'Day, Thomas F. The Sociology of Religion. Englewood
    Cliffs, N.J.: Prentice_hall, 1966.

Orsini, Joseph E. Hear My Confession. Plainfield,
    N.J.: Logos International, 1971.

Pelikan, Jaroslav. The Riddle of Roman Catholicism.
    New York: Abingdon Press, 1969.

Peters, Edward H., ed. De Ecclesia: The Constitution
    on the Church of Vatican Council II. Glen Rock,
    N.J.: Deus Books, 1965.

136

Quebedeaux, Richard. The New Charismatics. Garden
    City, New York: Doubleday & Co., 1976.

Rahner, Karl. The Dynamic Element in the Church.
    New York: Herder & Herder, 1964.

_____ and Vorgrimler, eds. Theological Dictionary.
    Translated by Richard Strachan. New York:
    Herder & Herder, 1965.

Ranaghan, Kevin and Dorothy, eds. As the Spirit
    Leads Us. New York: Paulist Press, 1971.

_____. Catholic Pentecostals. New York: Paulist
    Press, 1969.

Ratzinger, Joseph. Theological Highlights of Vatican
    II. New York: Paulist Press, 1966.

Sherrill, John L. They Speak With Other Tongues.
    Old Tappan, N.J.: Spire Books, 1964.

Stephanou, Eusebius A. The Charismatic Renewal in
    the Orthodox Church. Fort Wayne, Ind.:
    Logos Ministry for Orthodox Renewal, 1976.

Suave, Paul. Prompted by the Spirit. Montreal:
    Beauchemin, 1974.

Suenens, Leon Joseph. A New Pentecost? New York:
    Seabury Press, 1975.

_____. "The Charismatic Dimension of the Church."
    Council Speeches of Vatican II. Edited by
    Yves Congar, Hans Kung and Daniel O'Hanlon.
    New York: Paulist Press, 1964.

_____. Ecumenism and Charismatic Renewal:
    Theological and Pastoral Orientations. Ann
    Arbor: Servant Books, 1978.

_____. Essays on Renewal. Ann Arbor: Servant
    Books, 1977.

Synan, Vinson, ed. Aspects of Pentecostal-Charis-
      matic Origins. Plainfield, N.J.: Logos
      International, 1975.

_____. The Holiness-Pentecostal Movement in the
      United States. Grand Rapids: Wm. B. Eerdmans
      Publishing Co., 1971.

Theological and Pastoral Orientations on the Catholic
      Charismatic Renewal. Notre Dame, Ind.: Word
      of Life, 1974.

Tinsley, E.J. "Monasticism" in A Dictionary of
      Christian Theology. Edited by Alan Richardson.
      Philadelphia: Westminister Press, 1969.

Vorgrimler, Herbert. Karl Rahner: His Life, Thought
      and Works. Translated by Edward Quinn.
      London: Burns & Oates, 1965.

Wells, David F. Revolution in Rome. Downers Grove,
      Ill.: InterVarsity Press, 1972.

Wilkerson, David. The Vision. Old Tappan, N.J.:
      Fleming H. Revell, 1974.

Wills, Gary. Bare Ruined Choirs: Doubt, Prophecy,
      and Radical Religion. New York: Delta
      Books, 1971.

Wojytla, Karol. "Commentary on Decree on the Aposto-
      late of the Laity." The Sixteen Documents
      of Vatican II. Compiled by J.L. Gonzales.
      Boston: Daughter's of St. Paul, n.d.

Zablocki, Benjamin. The Joyful Community. Baltimore,
      Md.: Penguin Books, 1971.

                        Pamphlets

Clark, Stephen B. Baptized in the Spirit. Pecos,
      N.M.: Dove Publishers, 1970.

_____. Confirmation and "The Baptism of the Holy
      Spirit". Pecos, N.M.: Dove Publishers, 1969.

_____. Spiritual Gifts. Pecos, N.M.: Dove Publishers, 1969

Committee for Pastoral Research and Practices. Statement on Catholic Charismatic Renewal. Washington, D.C.: U.S. Catholic Conference, 1975.

Finding New Life in the Spirit: A Guidebook for the Life in the Spirit Seminars. Notre Dame, Ind.: Charismatic Renewal Services, 1972.

Ford, J. Massyngberde. The Pentecostal Experience. New York: Paulist Press, 1970.

Harper, Michael. Power for the Body of Christ. Plainfield, N.J.: Logos Books, 1964.

Introduction to the Catholic Charismatic Renewal. Notre Dame, Ind.: Charismatic Renewal Services, n.d.

McDonnell, Kilian, and Bittlinger, Arnold. The Baptism in the Holy Spirit as an Ecumenical Problem. Notre Dame, Ind.: Charismatic Renewal Services, 1972.

_____. Catholic Pentecostalism: Problems in Evaluation. Pecos, N.M.: Dove Publishers, 1970.

_____. Statement of the Theological Basis of the Catholic Charismatic Renewal. Pecos, N.M.: Dove Publishers, 1970.

Jesus Christ is the Light of the World: 1974 International Conference on the Charismatic Renewal in the Catholic Church. Notre Dame, Ind.: Charismatic Renewal Services, 1974.

Message of the Canadian Bishops. Charismatic Renewal. Ontario: Canadian Catholic Conference. Publishing Service, 1975.

O'Connor, Edward D. The Laying on of Hands. Pecos, N.M.: Dove Publishers, 1969.

139

_____. _Pentecost in the Catholic Church_. Pecos,
N.M.: Dove Publishers, 1970.

_____. _Pentecost in the Modern World_. Notre Dame,
Ind.: Ave Maria Press, 1972.

Pfaller, Louis and Alberts, Larry J. _Mary is Pentecostal_.
Pecos, N.M.: Dove Publishers, 1973.

Ranaghan, Kevin. _The Lord, the Spirit and the Church_.
Notre Dame, Ind.: Charismatic Renewal
Services, 1973.

Whitney, Jill. _The Charismatic Renewal--What's It
All About?_ Paper for the press at the 1974
International Charismatic Convention, Notre
Dame, Ind., March 4, 1974.

_____. _Facts for the Press_. Paper for the press
at the 1976 Continental Conference of the
Charismatic Renewal in the Catholic Church.
Notre Dame, Ind., May 28-30, 1976.

Periodicals

Bell, Bob. "Charismatic Communities: Questions and
Cautions." _New Covenant_, July, 1973, p. 4.

Bergquist, S.L. "Revival of Glossolalia Practices
in the Catholic Church: Its Sociological
Implications." _Perkins School of Theology
Journal_ 27 (Summer 1973).

Fiske, Edward B. "Look Who's Speaking in Tongues
Now." Christian Herald. Sept. 1970, pp. 7-13.

Ford, J. Massyngberde. "The Diaconate and the Neo-
Pentecostal Renewal Within the Catholic
Church." _American Ecclesiastical Review_ 16
(Feb. 1972):84-93.

_____. "Fly United--But Not in Too Close For-
mation: Reflections on the Catholic Pentecostal Movement." _Spiritual Life_ 17
(Spring 1971:12-20.

_____. "Pentecostal Poise or Docetic Charis-
        matics?" Spiritual Life 17 (Spring 1973):
        32-47.

_____. "Toward a Theology of 'Speaking in
        Tongues'." Theological Studies 32 (March 1971):
        3-29.

Gelpi, Donald, "Charismatic Renewal: Problems,
        Possibilities." National Catholic Reporter,
        Aug. 3, 1973, pp. 7,14.

Ghezzi, Bertil. "The End of the Catholic Pentecostal
        Movement." Sign 51 (Nov. 1971):10-12.

Gibeau, Dawn. "Pentecostals: They Speak of the
        Spirit and Some Speak in Tongues." National
        Catholic Reporter, Jan. 22, 1973, p. 64.

Grace, Edward. "Can John Paul Reform the Vatican?"
        Christian Century, Jan. 31, 1979, p. 102.

Greeley, Mary Ellen. "Charismatics and Noncharis-
        matics, A Comparison." Review for Religious
        33 (Feb. 1974):316-35.

Harper, Michael. "Charismatic Renewal: A New Ecumen-
        ism?" One In Christ 9 (no. 1, 1973):59-65.

Harsh, Kathleen. "Charismatics Live Together." South
        Bend Tribune, 7 Aug. 1977, p. 30.

Hollenweger, Walter. "Pentecostalism's Contribution
        to the World Church." Theology Digest 19
        (Spring 1971):54-57.

Hulen, David. "Charismatic Drive Big Business."
        South Bend Tribune, 7 Aug. 1977.

Landers, Ann. "How Many Priests, Nuns Have Quit?"
        Houston Chronicle, 16 March 1979, p. 8.

Likoudis, James. "The Pentecostalism Controversy."
        Social Justice Review, Sept. 1973, pp. 148-157.

Martin, Ralph. "About This Issue." New Covenant,
    July 1973, p. 2.

McDonald, H. Dermot. "What is meant by Religious
    Experience?" Vox Evangelica, 1963 ed. London
    Bible College, p. 68.

McDonnell, Kilian. "The Ideology of Pentecostal
    Conversion." Journal of Ecumenical Studies 5
    (Winter, 1968):105-26.

_____. "Distinguishing Characteristics of the
    Charismatic-Pentecostal Spirituality."
    One in Christ 10 (1974):122-23.

McHale, John V. "The Charismatic Renewal Movement."
    The Furrow 24 (May 1973):259-71.

Pikell, Donald E. "Speaking in Tongues." Ligourian 60
    (Spring, 1972): 46-49.

"Pope Paul's Statement to Leaders in the Charismatic
    Renewal--Oct. 10, 1973. "New Covenant,"
    Dec. 1973, p. 5.

"Pope Renews Mandate Given to Cardinal Suenens."
    New Covenant, April, 1979, p. 20.

Smith, Whitney, "Charismatics: United or Hell-Bent
    for Schism." South Bend Tribune, 7 July 1977.

Suenens, Leon Joseph. "The Pentecostal Movement: An
    Interview." Tablet 227 (18 Aug. 1973):789-91.

"Survey Rates Pentecostals High on Piety, Low on
    Social Action." National Catholic Reporter,
    8 June 1973, p. 3.

Tugwell, Simon. "Reflections on the Pentecostal
    Doctrine of 'Baptism in the Holy Spirit',"
    in two parts. Heythrop Journal 13 (July 1972):
    268-81 and 14 (Oct. 1972):402-14.

Van Dusen, Henry P. "Force's Lessons for Others."
Life, 9 June 1958, pp. 122-24.

Taped Materials

Press Conferences

Catholic Charismatic Renewal Service Committee.
Hal Cohen, Paul DeCelles and Ralph Martin.
University of Notre Dame, 16 June 1974.

Covenant Communities: What's Happening in the Renewal
Today. South Bend, Ind., 29 May 1976.

Ecumenism. Steve Clark, Robert Frost, Joseph C.
McKinney, University of Notre Dame, 16 June
1974.

Healing. Francis MacNutt, Mike Scanlan, Tom Forrest
and Barbara Schlemon. University of Notre
Dame, 15 June 1974.

International Charismatic Renewal. Leon Joseph
Suenens, Ralph Martin, Bernardin Schneider
and Tom Flynn. University of Notre Dame,
15 June 1974.

Lectures

Clark, Stephen. Salvation (two tapes). Maria
Immaculata Prayer Group. Chicago, Ill., n.d.

_____. Scripture and Tradition. Lecture delivered
at the 1974 International Conference on the
Charismatic Renewal in the Catholic Church.
University of Notre Dame, 16 June 1974.

_____. Word Gifts: Teaching. Maria Immaculata
Prayer Group, Chicago, Ill., n.d.

Hoyer, George. Preaching the Types of Salvation
History of Secularized Christians. The 1978
Institute of Liturgical Studies. Valparaiso
University, Valparaiso, Inc., 2 Feb. 1978.

143

McDonnell Kilian. _Reflections on Classical Pentecostal-ism._ Notre Dame, Ind.: Charismatic Renewal Services, 1973.

Ranaghan, Devin. _The First Seven Years of the Catholic Charismatic Renewal._ Notre Dame, Ind.: Charismatic Renewal Services, 1973.

Yokum, Bruce. _Word Gifts: Prophecy._ Maria Immaculata Prayer Group. Chicago, Ill., n.d.

Meetings & Conventions

1976 Continental Conference on the Charismatic Renewal in the Catholic Church. University of Notre Dame, Notre Dame, Ind., May 28-30, 1976.

1978 Institute of Liturgical Studies. Valparaiso University, Valparaiso, Ind., Feb. 2-4, 1978.

1974 International Conference on the Charismatic Renewal in the Catholic Church. University of Notre Dame, Notre Dame, Ind., March 4-6, 1974.

Interviews

Bowton, John and Jill. South Bend, Ind., 11 Nov. 1975.

Ford, J. Massyngberde. South Bend, Ind., 13 June 1976.

Kohler, Kerry. South Bend, Ind., 16 Oct., 20 Oct., 1977, 16 Nov. 1977.

Martin, Ralph. South Bend, Ind., 29 May 1976.

Rahner, Karl. Chicago, Ill., 7 Nov. 1974.

Stayton, Timothy. Valparaiso University, 2 Feb. 1978.